D0196912

Preventing Violence

Preventing Violence

James Gilligan

Thames & Hudson

"The only way to get kids not to hurt each other is to get kids not to want to hurt each other."

Russell Novotny, a recent high school graduate, commenting on the emphasis on metal detectors and security guards as the main response to a recent epidemic of mass murders in American high schools (Adrian LeBlanc, "The Outsiders," *New York Times Magazine*, August, 1999)

"Using the cops to crack crime is like taking aspirin for a brain tumor."

Philip Marlowe, in Raymond Chandler's *The Long Goodbye*

First published in paperback in the United States of America in 2001 by Thames & Hudson Inc., 500 Fifth Avenue, New York, New York 10110

Library of Congress Catalog Card Number 00-108865
ISBN 0-500-28278-1

Printed and bound in Slovenia by Mladinska Knjiga

Contents

INTRODUCTION TWO APPROACHES TO PREVENTING VIOLENCE 7

CHAPTER 1 SHAME AND THE DEATH OF THE SELF 29

CHAPTER 2 THE SOCIAL CAUSES OF VIOLENCE 38

CHAPTER 3 VIOLENCE AS PROOF OF MASCULINITY 56

CHAPTER 4 A NEW THEORY OF VIOLENCE 66

CHAPTER 5 HOW TO CREATE LESS VIOLENT SOCIETIES 80

CHAPTER 6 SECONDARY PREVENTION:
EARLY INTERVENTION 107

CHAPTER 7 TERTIARY PREVENTION:
THERAPEUTIC INTERVENTION 114

CHAPTER 8 WHO BENEFITS FROM VIOLENCE? 131

SELECT BIBLIOGRAPHY AND SOURCES 139

INDEX 142

TWO APPROACHES TO PREVENTING VIOLENCE

For the past four millennia, since the time of the first law-givers—Hammurabi and Moses, Drakon and Solon, Plato and Aristotle, Cicero and Justinian—humanity has been engaged in a great social experiment, testing the hypothesis that we could prevent violence, or at least diminish its scale and intensity, by labeling it "evil" and "criminal"; ordering people not to engage in it; and then, when they commit acts of violence anyway, retaliating with more violence of our own, which we call "punishment" and "justice." Now, four thousand years is long enough to test any hypothesis, and the results of this experiment have been in for a long time: this means of attempting to prevent violence, which I will call the traditional *moral and legal* approach, far from solving the problem of violence, or even diminishing the threat it poses to our continued survival, has in fact been followed by a continued escalation of the frequency and intensity of violence, to the point that the century we have just survived has been the bloodiest in all human history, with more humans killing other humans than in all previous centuries combined. Worse yet, we have now achieved, through a deliberate effort, the technological ability to kill everyone on earth, thus becoming the first species in evolutionary history to be in danger of bringing about its own extinction—unless we can increase our ability to prevent violence far more effectively than we have for the past four thousand years.

Given that the approach used for the past four millennia has been such a total failure—indeed, has been so counter-productive, resulting in more rather than less violence—the beginning of a new millennium would seem to be an auspicious moment to consider replacing that ancient strategy with a radically new and different one. That is why I welcomed the invitation to contribute to this series of books on the major challenges and opportunities, the major problems and most promising solutions, that we can anticipate during the coming millennium, and to bring to bear on the most important problem a perspective derived from the human sciences.

Many judges and legal scholars, and even some legislators, agree that there is a need to question many of the law's traditional assumptions and practices, and are working to bring the criminal justice system into the twenty-first century. For example, there are many experiments with attempts to replace retributive with restorative justice, and to develop new concepts such as therapeutic jurisprudence, alternative sentencing schemes, drug courts, and so on, as I will discuss at greater length in Chapter 7. On a larger scale, many national governments and even international bodies like the United Nations and the International Criminal Tribunal in The Hague are trying to discover, or invent, new bases for negotiating an end to collective violence in all its forms—genocide, war crimes, totalitarianism, racial discrimination, "ethnic cleansing," and so on; for repairing the physical and psychological trauma those forms of violence leave in their wake; and for preventing new outbreaks of them, through "truth and reconciliation" commissions, selective amnesty policies, peacekeeping missions, abandonment of traditional notions of national sovereignty, and so on. They are engaging in these social and legal experiments in the only way that we have ever been able to develop successful new strategies for living together—namely, slowly, painfully, controversially, by trial and error, and in an atmosphere of humility and open debate rather than of vengeance and self-righteousness.

In other words, the issue I am raising here is not a debate between law and psychiatry as much as a debate that is going on within the law itself, which to its credit has given it more attention than most psychiatrists have, with many judges, law schools, and schools of government and public policy welcoming contributions from several different disciplines. Many of the judges, attorneys, government officials, legislators, law enforcement professionals and prison administrators with whom I have worked over the past thirty years are clearly aware of the massive shortcomings and failures of our traditional ways of attempting to cope with the dangers to which the human propensity for violence exposes us all. The only question is: with what can we replace them? That is what I will try to outline in what follows.

In this short book, I will make no attempt to provide a comprehensive survey of the many specific community initiatives proposed for preventing violence. Excellent compendia and summaries are already available (e.g. Sherman, et al., *Preventing Crime*, 1997; Tonry and Farrington, *Building a Safer Society*, 1995; Tolan and Guerra, *What Works in Reducing Adolescent Violence*, 1998). They can also be found increasingly, on the internet: for example, on its website, http://www.colorado.edu/cspv/blueprints/index.html, the Center for the Study and Prevention of Violence at the University of Colorado, Boulder, has identified ten highly effective violence prevention programs, sufficient to provide a nucleus for a national violence prevention initiative, and seventeen promising programs. Nor have I attempted to write a "how-to" or "cookbook" approach, summarizing step-by-step recipes for putting together any one program.

I have two worries about much of what passes for "violence prevention" in the literature on this subject (apart from such thoughtful treatments as those referred to above). The first is that we are in danger of forgetting that when we talk about preventing violence, we are not talking about something that can be solved with gimmicks; we are not talking about "techniques." We are talking about *whether, and how, we and other human beings can learn to live with each other, and even to want to live with each other*—and I mean live as opposed to die, for that is the only other choice where violence is concerned. But that is too profound a question to be answered by anything other than a radical rethinking of the most basic principles on which our social life is based. We are in danger of not seeing the forest—or, more to the point, of not noticing that the forest as a whole is being destroyed as we talk—if we get distracted by examining a thousand different little trees. As David Downes has written in *Crime* (1995):

Some social crime-prevention projects have been mounted, but—despite some successes—they tend to be too localized, short-term and underfunded to make a lasting impact. Tony Blair's formulation—"Tough on crime, tough on the causes of crime"—is greatly to be preferred, but rests on the premiss that we can sort out the confusion about what those causes are and then agree on how to tackle them. Meanwhile, being tough on crime [the traditional moral and legal approach, which is more expensive, and if anything exacerbates the problem] takes priority by default.

You cannot stop a hemorrhage with Band-Aids, however many you apply; for a hemorrhage, you need major surgery. And I worry that as we fritter away our time and energies debating the minutiae of small-scale do-it-yourself-type community initiatives, the patient will bleed to death. Naturally, those who do not want major change would prefer to restrict the conversation to timid, half-hearted preventive efforts. They maintain that we cannot afford to do what preventing violence will require, or that the voters, who in the meantime are not being educated, will not support it—so that this whole argument becomes a self-fulfilling prophecy. Meanwhile, no expense or cruelty is spared in the effort to inflict as much pain as possible on those whom we use as scapegoats for our own massive failure to create a real family of humankind, namely, a viable social and economic system.

As the authors of one of the best and most comprehensive evaluations of violence-prevention programs put it:

> Communities are the central institution for crime prevention, the stage on which all other institutions perform. Families, schools, labor markets, retail establishments, police, and corrections must confront the consequences of community life. Much of the success or failure of these other institutions is affected by the community context in which they operate. Our nation's ability to prevent serious violent crime may depend heavily on our ability to help reshape community life. . . . The causes correlated with serious crime are basic and interconnected, while the programs are superficial and piecemeal. . . . For most of this century, community crime prevention programs have failed to tackle the governmental policies and market forces that fuel inner-city violence. . . . Ironically, a central tenet of community

prevention programs has been the empowerment of local community leaders to design and implement their own crime prevention strategies. This philosophy may amount to throwing people overboard and then letting them design their own life preserver. The scientific literature shows that the policies and market forces causing criminogenic community structures and cultures are beyond the control of neighborhood residents, and that "empowerment" does not include the power to change those policies. . . . It is one thing, for example, for tenants to manage the security guards in a public housing project. It is another thing entirely to let tenants design a new public housing policy and determine where in a metropolitan area households with public housing support will live. . . . Thus the major causes of community crime problems are like handcuffs locking a community into a high crime rate. The most frequently evaluated community-based crime prevention programs do not attempt to break those handcuffs. Rather, they operate inside those constraints, attempting "small wins" within the limited range of risk factors they can manipulate. But until the handcuffs of race-based politics themselves are unlocked, many analysts expect relatively few major improvements from programs addressing only the symptoms of those constraints.

(Sherman, et al., *Preventing Crime*)

Or, to paraphrase Jeremiah, our false prophets cry, "Community, community," but we have no community! Our first task, then, before we can even begin to think about preventing violence, is to learn how to create something that would actually be a community. That is why I have concentrated in this book on developing *a new way of thinking* about preventing violence, rather than simply providing recipes as to how to replicate one program or another tried somewhere already. The gift of a fish only feeds us for a day, and we really need to learn how to fish. So instead of limiting myself to the *facts* of what people have done so far, I will attempt to see if we can discover some basic *principles* underlying the causes and prevention of violence, so that we will all be in a better position to originate new ideas and approaches, and to evaluate those that have already been proposed or implemented by others, as well as those that will only exist in the future.

One more century in which the human capacity to commit individual murders and other crimes, and also mass murder, genocide and war crimes, increases as explosively as it did during the past century, and we may not survive for as long as another millennium. Either we will learn to end violence as a means of resolving disputes and pursuing goals during the coming century, or it will end us. The old approach—the traditional moral and legal approach—has not only failed to solve the problem, it has actually made it worse. Its failure is so total that the question of whether or not we should continue it is no longer even debatable; the moral and legal approach is not merely bankrupt theoretically, it is positively dangerous in practical terms. Why has the traditional approach been such a total failure? There are many reasons, of which I will mention two.

Is the Criminal Law Based on a Huge Mistake?

The first reason is that we cannot learn what *causes* violence and how we could *prevent* it as long as we are thinking in the traditional moral and legal terms. The only questions that this way of thinking can ask take the form: "How *evil* (or heroic) was this particular act of violence, and how much *punishment* (or reward) does the person who did it *deserve*?" But even if it were possible to gain the knowledge that would be necessary to answer those questions (which it is not), answers would still not help us in the least to understand either what *causes* violence or how we could *prevent* it—these are *empirical* not *moral* questions. It is only by approaching violence from the point of view of empirical disciplines, as a problem in *public health and preventive medicine, including social and preventive psychiatry and psychology*, that we can acquire knowledge as to the *causes and prevention* of violence—by engaging in clinical, experimental, and epidemiological research on violent and non-violent behavior, the people who behave in those ways, and the circumstances under which they do so.

I have devoted much of my professional life to doing exactly that, and this book about preventing violence, like its predecessor on the causes of violence (Gilligan, *Violence*, 1996), will consist of summarizing for you what I saw and heard in the course of more than thirty years of participating in, directing, and evaluating violence prevention programs with the most violent people that our society produces. In order to conduct this research, I used as my "laboratory," so to speak, one institution in our society which contains, by deliberate purpose, a "pure culture" of violence—namely, the prison. Prisons are intended, after all, as the receptacles in which we isolate those individuals (mostly men) whom we have identified as the most extremely and unacceptably violent. My friends and colleagues often asked me why I chose to work in such terrible places as prisons and the prison mental hospital, and with patients who are dangerous and with whom it is hard to sympathize, when I already had a comfortable private practice and a teaching position at the Harvard Medical School. I would answer by paraphrasing the bank-robber Willie Sutton, who replied, when asked why he robbed banks, "Because that's where the money is." I worked in the prisons because that's where the violence is; it's where the violent people are. And that was what I was interested in and wanted to understand better. I do not know how one could learn why people become violent, or what we can do to prevent violence, except by working on those problems with violent people. I can think of no better laboratory in which to investigate those subjects, and in which to observe at first hand—from "the inside," literally—the whole apparatus of crime and punishment and the criminal justice system.

So when I contrast the traditional moral and legal way of thinking with the approach of public health and preventive medicine, I am not speculating or speaking as a philosopher engaging in abstract theorizing. This is an intensely practical and down-to-earth difference, with real consequences for real people, with which I was confronted on a daily basis for many years. For example, I have testified in scores of court-room trials of people charged with murder and other violent crimes, as an "expert witness" whose job was to perform psychiatric evaluations of the defendants. I could not have had a more intensive exposure to the differences in the kinds of questions that are asked by the legal system when we approach violence as a moral and legal problem (e.g. "Does this defendant have an 'evil mind,' a *mens rea*?"—the moral value judgment that is a precondition for a finding of legal guilt), versus the kinds of questions we are prompted to ask when we think of violence as a problem in public health and preventive medicine ("What led this man to commit such a violent act—i.e. what interaction of biological, psychological and social forces caused him to harm someone, and what can we do to decrease the likelihood that he and others will behave that way in the future?")

There were times in the courtrooms and prisons in which I did my work when I felt as though I had somehow been transported by mistake back into the Middle Ages, when people still thought that evil (like its mythical embodiment and namesake, the devil) was an objective thing that actually existed independently of our subjective feelings and thoughts, rather than a word we all too often use to rationalize, justify, and conceal, from ourselves and others, our own violence toward those we hate and wish to punish. The more we have taken that approach to the "evil minds" in our midst, the people we call criminals, the more we have acted like medieval inquisitors who believed that we could exorcise this evil from our midst only by torturing all the evil people, burying them alive, or burning them at the stake (for which we in the U.S. today have substituted stun guns, total solitary confinement for years at a time in underground tombs called "supermax" prisons, and electric chairs. All this so that we could call ourselves "compassionate" executioners rather than recognizing how close we are to engaging in our own version of the dungeon, torture chamber and *auto-da-fé* of times past).

Once we have labeled someone as "evil" there is often no limit to the cruelty and violence we can feel justified in administering to him, including the forms of torture and human sacrifice to which I have just referred, all of which are increasingly widely mandated by American legislatures, enforced by American courts, and practiced in American prisons, toward men, women and, increasingly, children and the retarded—all in the name of morality, law and justice. Because of its continuing and even increasing use of prolonged total solitary confinement, stun guns and capital punishment, the U.S. criminal justice system was condemned in May 2000 by the United Nations Committee Against Torture, and has many times been found in violation of the U.N.'s Minimum Standards for the Treatment of Prisoners. Ironically, the criminals I see evaluate and justify their own violence—the torture and hostage-taking and human sacrifices they commit—by means of exactly the same kinds of moral value judgments that our legal system uses: "the bitch deserved it" or "the son of a bitch deserved it."

For a quarter of a century, from 1967 through 1992, I worked in the Massachusetts prisons, first as a psychotherapist (as part of my training in psychiatry), then as Medical Director of the prison mental hospital (for the "criminally insane"), and finally as Director of Mental Health Services for the prison system as a whole. During the 1970s, I directed a team of mental health professionals from a teaching hospital of the Harvard Medical School, where I was Director of the Institute of Law and Psychiatry, in providing psychiatric evaluations and treatment at the prison mental hospital. During that same time, the Massachusetts prisons, in which we had no presence, were a virtual war zone. In the 600-man maximum security prison (or maximum insecurity prison, as we called it), in addition to riots, there were periods in which there was an average of a murder a month and a suicide every six weeks; the decade as a whole ended with a total of more than a hundred violent deaths at that one prison alone. And throughout all the prisons there was an epidemic of homicides, suicides, riots, arson, gang rapes, hostage-taking, and self-mutilation (prisoners gouging their eyes out, cutting off their genitals, pulling out their toenails, swallowing razor blades), in which prisoners, prison staff and visitors were being killed or grievously injured.

In response to those conditions, lawyers representing inmates who had been injured or killed sued the state prison authorities in Federal Court. The investigation that followed determined that much of this violence was precipitated by untreated, undiagnosed mental illness, much of which was itself precipitated or at least exacerbated by conditions within the prisons—the sensory deprivation and social isolation produced by prolonged solitary confinement; the pervasive atmosphere of terror and overwhelming stress leading to post-traumatic symptoms and syndromes; and a great deal of pre-existing, chronic mental illness that had simply never been diagnosed or treated. Many of those who committed homicide and/or suicide had been actively hallucinating, delusional, or showing other symptoms of psychosis at the time of their violence. But it would hardly be an exaggeration to say that in such a violent environment the prisoners would almost have to be "paranoid" in order to be in touch with reality; they really did have enemies, and they really were in danger. In fact, if one were trying design a system for deliberately making people paranoid and violent, one could hardly have come up with a more successful model. Because of the self-fulfilling nature of persecutory delusions—the person who believes he is surrounded by enemies behaving in such a hostile, aggressive way that others see him as their enemy and respond in kind—the whole situation became a vicious circle, violence leading to paranoia leading to more violence. (A familiar scenario for anyone who follows international relations and world politics—which is one reason why lessons learned in this microcosm may be relevant on a macrocosmic scale.)

The outcome of the class-action suit was a consent decree in which the Department of Correction asked us to expand our provision of psychiatric services from the mental hospital to the entire prison system, and I became responsible for directing this program. Because of that complicated history, our mandate included not only the treatment of mental illness but, in effect, the prevention of violence; and our "patients" became not only the individuals whom we evaluated and treated, but the prison system itself. That is, the whole project became an exercise not just in clinical but also in social, community and preventive psychiatry aimed at healing the pathology at the heart of the criminal justice system itself.

I directed the program for ten years, setting up a system of psychiatric emergency rooms and mental health clinics in each prison, and staffing them with members of the Medical School faculty who were available in person or on call around the clock to provide crisis interventions, protective custody, suicide precautions, psychotherapy, psychopharmacology, transfers of prisoners to and from the prison mental hospital, and constant consultations to and training of the correctional staff. What were the results? We found that it is possible to prevent violence virtually anywhere, in even the most violent of environments, if you want to badly enough and are willing to devote sufficient time and effort to the task. During the first five years of our program, while we were still recruiting and training staff to work in this unique environment, and learning from our own mistakes, there were no riots at any prison, though there were two serious hostage-taking incidents (both of which we were able to resolve without any deaths). No staff members or visitors were killed, though seven inmates (throughout the prison system as a whole) died from homicide or suicide. During the second five years, there were no riots, no hostage-taking, and a total of one homicide and two suicides throughout the state prison system; that is, there were some full years with no violent deaths in any of the prisons.

We can consider this program as an experimental confirmation of the hypothesis that it is possible to prevent all or almost all occurrences of the most serious forms of violence year after year, even in the most violent environments and among the most violent people in our society. That is the first principle it illustrated.

The second principle is that it is possible to succeed at preventing violence only to the extent that we abolish the traditional moral and legal approach, which the prisons had been following up to that time. The more violent an inmate was, the more severely he would be punished, and the more severely he was punished, the more violent he would become. This endless, mutually self-defeating vicious circle kept both inmates and prison officers in a chronic state of war with each other—which was the opposite of what they both said they wanted. And of course we make the same mistake on the scale of society as a whole as in that microcosm of our society called a prison: the more violent people are in the community the more severely we punish them (even killing some of them, as an example to the others), and the more severely we punish them, the more violent they become (since they have learned to follow our own violent example). In place of moral condemnation and punishment, we attempted to learn how to understand why the prisoners (and officers) were behaving as they were, and to use that as the basis for all our interventions. Over time we evolved several basic principles that governed our interactions with them, the most important of which I have summarized in Chapter 7.

The second reason that the traditional moral and legal approach to violence actually stimulates violence, rather than preventing it, is because it is based on one huge mistake—namely, an unquestioned assumption, which is not merely a factual error, but actually reverses the truth. The criminal justice system, and all the other institutions in our society, to the extent that they are based on moral ways of thinking, have not recognized or been capable of recognizing that this assumption is mistaken because it cannot be examined, criticized, or tested as long as one is thinking in moral terms—for it is not a moral assumption. Rather, it is an *empirical* assumption—namely, the assumption that *punishing* those who commit violent acts will deter them and others from committing such acts in the future; in other words, the assumption that *punishment (the deliberate infliction of pain) prevents violence.* As long as we restrict ourselves to thinking in the traditional terms about punishment as a response to crime and violence (including war crimes), we find that the only kinds of questions we can ask are those that employ moral categories rather than empirical ones, such as, "Did the person *deserve* that punishment," or, "Was it a *just* punishment?" However, when one tests against empirical data the assumption that punishment will prevent violence, by examining how people who are punished actually behave, one finds that far from preventing violence, *punishment is the most powerful stimulus to violent behavior that we have yet discovered* (as I will document in Chapter 7, and as I have discussed in more detail in my article "Punishment and Violence," 2000). Punishment does not *prevent* violence, it *causes* it, in addition to being a form of it. So it is not surprising that the moral and legal approach to violence has been followed by four millennia of constantly increasing levels of violence.

Violence as a Public Health Problem

But if punishment does not prevent violence, what does? In order to find answers to that question, to which most of the rest of this book will be devoted, it will be helpful, even necessary, to think about violence not as a moral and legal problem, but as a problem in public health and preventive medicine. We treat illnesses, we do not punish them. Bertrand Russell in *Roads to Freedom* (1918) summarized the implications of that difference in approach in these words:

> When a man is suffering from an infectious disease, he is a danger to the community, and it is necessary to restrict his liberty of movement. But no one associates any idea of guilt with such a situation. On the contrary, he is an object of commiseration to his friends. Such steps as science recommends are taken to cure him of his disease, and he submits as a rule without reluctance to the curtailment of liberty involved meanwhile. The same method in spirit ought to be shown in the treatment of what is called "crime."

I will use the terms disease, illness, and pathology to refer to any force or process within an organism or species that tends to bring death or disability to the organism, or extinction to the species. Violence in all of the forms just mentioned is, by that definition, a manifestation, form, or symptom of pathology or illness, at least as much as cancer and heart disease are, for it is a force or process within members of the human species that tends to bring death, disability, and potentially even extinction (self-extinction) to them. This is true even though defensive violence can be a means (and in some circumstances may be the only means) of saving one's life, or the lives of other potential victims of an aggressor. But if defensive violence can save life, how can it also be a symptom of pathology or illness? The answer is that it is a symptom of the pathology of the aggressor (i.e. it is caused and made necessary by the aggressor's behavior). The aggressor's violence meets my definition of pathology—it not only tends to bring injury or death to the victim, it also increases the risk of injury or death to the perpetrator (whose aggression is likely to provoke violence from the people being attacked). Those who live by the sword die by the sword —and usually at a younger age than those who are not habitually violent—shown by the repeated (and hardly surprising) observation that the life-span of recurrently violent people is, on average, shorter than that of non-violent ones. That is, in fact, one of the most direct forms of evidence that violence is a manifestation of disease: it shortens the life-span (on average) just as other diseases do, and it therefore conforms to my definition of disease. Preventing aggressive violence means preventing both forms of violence: we prevent *defensive* violence whenever we prevent *aggressive* violence.

This book on preventing violence can be considered as a sequel to my earlier book (1996) in which I discussed the causes of violence. It is the completion of the project that I began with that book. The first and most efficient step toward learning how to prevent any health problem is, when at all possible, to discover what causes it, so that we know what causes need to be removed or neutralized. In the first few chapters I will recapitulate the conclusions regarding the causes of violence that I discussed at greater length in my earlier book. Once we know the causes, we can apply that knowledge to the issue of prevention in a very direct way, namely, by learning what we have been doing that causes violence, so that we will know what to stop doing. Implicit in this is the conclusion that violence does not occur spontaneously or without a cause, it only occurs when somebody does something that causes it. Therefore, all we need to do to prevent violence is to stop doing what we have been doing to cause it. If that idea seems strange at first, I would suggest that this is primarily because the causes of violence have not been sufficiently clearly recognized up to now. Like all illnesses, violence is caused by the interaction between biological, psychological and social determinants (Engel,"From Biomedical to Biopsychosocial," 1997)—a point that has important implications for prevention, namely, since there are multiple causes, there can also be multiple forms of prevention.

The basis of the public health approach is the distinction between three levels of prevention: primary, secondary and tertiary. Primary prevention refers to interventions that are applied to entire populations, regardless of their current health or relative risk of future illness. An example would be the discovery a hundred and fifty years ago that cleaning up the water supply and the sewer system was far more effective in protecting the entire population against certain infectious diseases than all the doctors, medicines, and hospitals in the world. It has also been shown that reductions in absolute poverty (raising populations above the subsistence level) and, once that has been achieved, reductions in relative poverty (achieving greater equality of wealth and income), have been far more responsible for the dramatic decreases in death rates and increases in longevity that have occurred over the past two centuries than improvements in medical treatment. It is still true, even in developed nations such as the U.K. and the U.S., that decreasing the degree of economic inequity between the rich and the poor is more effective in improving the health and longevity of the entire population than money spent on medical and surgical treatments (Wilkinson, *Unhealthy Societies*, 1996; Graubard, *Health and Wealth*, 1994; Black, et al., *The Black Report*, 1992). The U.S., for example, has the largest gaps in income and wealth between the rich and the poor of any developed country, one result of which is that even though it spends twice as much on healthcare as any of the others, it has among the lowest average life expectancies and the highest incidence of several major health problems. Exactly the same principles apply to the prevention of violence. I will summarize in Chapter 5 a number of social, economic and political policies that have been shown to be far more effective, in both absolute and relative (cost-effectiveness) terms, in protecting the population against epidemics of violence than all the police, prisons and punishments in the world. These are the principles of the primary prevention of violence.

Secondary prevention consists of interventions that are aimed at those subgroups in the population that are at higher than average risk of a particular illness, although they have not yet developed any actual symptoms or disabilities. Examples from preventive medicine would be intervening to lower high serum cholesterol or high blood pressure before the people being treated have had heart attacks or strokes. In Chapter 6 I will summarize some of the programs that have been shown to result in statistically significant reductions in the development of future violent behavior in people who are at higher than average risk both of being victimized by violence and of committing it themselves, but who have not yet been involved in any serious violence, compared with otherwise identical groups who have not had access to those programs. Groups that are at higher than average risk include, for example, children of unmarried, uneducated, poverty-stricken teenage mothers; survivors of child abuse or other family violence; people addicted to alcohol; residents of high-crime neighborhoods; people who are uneducated and unskilled; high school students after school lets out; and people who involve themselves in one way or another with the illegal drug trade.

Tertiary prevention refers to clinical medicine, as opposed to preventive medicine *per se*. It consists of the medical treatments or therapies that are given to those who have already become clinically ill with a particular illness, i.e. the treatments provided to sick people by doctors through medicines and surgical procedures, in clinics and hospitals. Why is treatment called prevention? Because its goal is to prevent an acute illness from becoming chronic or even fatal, and also to prevent the illness from spreading to people who do not yet have it (in the case of contagious diseases).

When we apply these concepts to the study of violence, we can see that the places where the tertiary prevention of violence is pursued are the criminal courts and the system of police, prisons and punishments, which traditionally have become involved only after someone has already become violent. I will discuss in Chapter 7 the kinds of programs and policies that have been demonstrated to work, and (just as importantly) the ones that have been shown to fail, in both "in-patient" settings (i.e. jails and prisons) and "out-patient" ones (e.g. community service, restorative justice, mandated out-patient treatment). I will also discuss the concept of an "anti-prison" as a radical replacement for traditional models of prison design and practice, and the reasons for recommending it.

Tertiary prevention is only needed when primary and secondary prevention have failed. Indeed, the need for tertiary prevention only exists to the degree that we have failed to provide sufficient primary and secondary prevention; the fact that there is a need for tertiary prevention at all is a sign of that failure. The old saying that an ounce of prevention is worth a pound of cure is demonstrably true. Applied to the subject of violence, we could say that an ounce of primary and secondary prevention are worth a megaton of cure. One of the major mistakes that both the medical healthcare system and the criminal justice system in the United States have made is to have invested far more money and personnel in tertiary than in primary and secondary prevention. For example, the U.S., the only developed nation that does not provide universal free health care for all its citizens, lags far behind even many Third World countries in rates of immunization of our children; and we lag behind every other developed nation in providing adequate prenatal care to expectant mothers, with the entirely predictable result that we spend many more billions of dollars in the often ineffective attempt to rescue premature babies than we would need to spend on providing much less expensive and far more effective prenatal care. As a result, the U.S. not only spends twice as high a percentage of its gross national product on healthcare as every other developed nation does, but also has higher rates of maternal and infant mortality and morbidity.

Exactly the same principle applies to the approach to violence in the U.S. The punishment and/or rehabilitation of those who have already been so damaged that they have become violent is also far more expensive and less effective than preventing violence in the first place, and it causes far more suffering, not only to the perpetrators but also to the victims. We spend incomparably more money on police, prisons, punishments and criminal courts than we do on providing the kinds of community services that have been demonstrated to achieve equal reductions in criminal violence for one-fifth of the price (see Chapter 7). As our prisons have become more and more crowded (and costly), the waiting lists in our substance-abuse treatment centers have become longer and longer—despite the fact (or rather, as I will argue in the final chapter of this book, because of the fact) that treatment is at least five times more effective than imprisonment, dollar for dollar, in preventing both substance abuse and the property crimes and violence associated with substance abuse.

The point I am making is that these policies are neither in our rational self-interest, nor are they defensible even in the "moral" terms in which they are usually defended (i.e. concern for victims, for the tax-payer, for law and order, for diminishing the harm done by drugs), for they only defeat us in our effort to achieve those ostensible goals. In that sense, the failure of U.S. criminal justice policies bears an eerie resemblance to the failure of our healthcare policies. Just as we spend more on health than any other developed nation and achieve worse results, so we spend more on our criminal justice system and also achieve worse results—in fact, dramatically worse. For example, our imprisonment rates are five to ten times higher than those of any other developed nation, and our death rates from murder are also five to ten times higher.

Now, what are the practical implications of applying the tripartite model of preventive medicine to the problem of violence? The first is that there are many different approaches to preventing violence, all of which help and all of which are worth pursuing. Unfortunately, the more powerful and efficient (cost-effective) they are, the more they are opposed by powerful political and economic forces, which is the major reason why violence continues to be such a major unsolved problem, especially in the U.S. and the developing world. For example, the polit-ical forces that oppose redistribution of wealth and income in the United States, not to mention the world as a whole, are much more powerful than those that support it, notwithstanding (or perhaps in part because of) the fact that no policy has been found to be more effective in preventing violence (as I will discuss in Chapters 5 and 8). Does that mean we cannot do anything unless or until the political cli-mate changes? The implication of the tripartite model of prevention that I am presenting here, which is simply the classical model of pre-ventive medicine throughout the world, is that if you cannot imple-ment one form of preventive medicine, you can implement another. In other words, if one or more of the strategies that I have listed under the category of primary prevention prove to be politically unfeasible for the foreseeable future (as I suspect almost all of them are at this point at the beginning of the third millennium CE), then we can always turn to those that might be more politically feasible now, including those categorized as secondary or tertiary prevention. And if and when the various primary prevention strategies become more politically viable, they can again be pursued. But there is never a point at which we need to be so paralyzed as to do nothing.

Another implication is that the prevention of violence is not an all-or-nothing matter. As with preventive medicine in general, success is almost always a matter of degree. Some illnesses, such as smallpox, it is true, have been completely eradicated throughout the world, and others, such as polio, in most developed countries. But even when we have not succeeded to that degree, any time we reduce the incidence of a disease even partially, we have prevented all the cases of it that would otherwise have occurred. The same applies to violence, which is why the title of this book, "preventing" violence, is not meant to imply that we have to eradicate *all* violence in order to speak of having prevented *some* of it.

On the other hand, I see no reason to rule out in advance the possibility of preventing at least the most dangerous and destructive forms of violence more or less completely rather than merely reducing them. One reason I say that is because a few remarkable societies—a very few, but the fact that they exist at all shows that it is possible—have in fact succeeded in preventing virtually all lethal and life-threatening violence, as I will discuss in Chapter 5. And I will maintain that there is in principle no reason why we could not do the same thing on a worldwide basis (which is not at all the same as predicting that we *will* do it). The reason that there is a difference between what we could do and what we may in fact do instead is because preventing violence is not the only goal, or even the main goal, that many people want to pursue. There are costs we would have to pay, and benefits we would have to sacrifice, in order even to attempt to prevent serious or lethal violence virtually completely, and we still might not know if our attempts were going to be successful until we had already paid a very heavy price. Violence brings very real advantages to many people, as I will discuss in the final chapter. It is not surprising that many would oppose the adoption of policies that would reduce the rates of violence.

I realize that to many people the idea that we know how to prevent violence at all, let alone the major and most destructive forms of it, may sound optimistic to the point of being utopian. That would be a misunderstanding of what I am saying, for two reasons.

A Question of Human Survival

The first is that I am not talking about a utopia, I am talking about survival. I am suggesting that learning how to prevent violence—not just slightly, but far more successfully than we have to now—is not an option, a luxury, which we may decide that we cannot afford, or that is not worth the price. Learning how to prevent violence is an absolute prerequisite for human survival during the coming century, the coming millennium, and the coming millennia. There may well be many different ways to succeed at this, and we already know that there are many different ways to fail (we have tried, and are still trying, many of the latter). But the research I will present in this book tends to support the conclusion that even though there may be a variety of potentially successful strategies for preventing violence, they are likely to have certain core principles in common, so that the variety of options may be compared to variations on a theme. And within the range of potentially successful options, it may well be that none would represent the kind of society that some people, even many people, would consider their idea of a utopia. But that is irrelevant to the point that I am making in this book. I am not designing a utopia, and not merely because one person's utopia is likely to be another's dystopia. I am talking about certain minimal characteristics that a society must possess in order not to self-destruct—and that is a very different and much less optimistic question than how to construct a utopia.

The second point is that I am not at all optimistic with regard to the likelihood that we will in fact mobilize the political will to do the things that I believe we would need to do in order to prevent further, increasingly genocidal catastrophes. When I say I am not optimistic about that, I do not mean that I pretend to know that it will happen, I simply mean that I see no basis for making the assumption that it will not. Japan and the nations of Western Europe had to go through unimaginable horrors before they mobilized the political will to make the radical changes in their political and economic systems that have enabled them for the half-century since the end of the last World War to pre-vent wars among themselves completely, and to prevent individual murders within their societies more completely, than any other large-scale civilizations in history. This they could do only by eliminating both poverty and dictatorship from their societies, the inequities of wealth and power that are among the main factors that lead men and nations to start wars and commit murders, more completely than any previous nations in history. Will the U.S., together with the rest of the developed and developing world, have to go through even more unimaginable horrors before we mobilize the collective political will to make the massive changes on a worldwide scale that will be necessary in order to prevent increasingly unsurvivable wars and genocidal mas-sacres? I do not pretend to know the answer to that question; I will only say that whoever has the confidence, the optimism and the utopi-anism to answer it in the negative must know something that I do not.

We have for all practical purposes eradicated some forms of vio-lence completely, at least in most places most of the time (such as can-nibalism and slavery). And a few remarkable small-scale societies, as I will discuss in Chapter 5, have succeeded in almost totally eradicating the major forms of lethal violence, such as murder and war, for decades or even centuries. But the major question that confronts us now is not whether we can be as successful as those societies have been in preventing violence, it is whether we can learn to prevent enough of it to ensure the survival of our societies themselves.

To say that we need to prevent violence if we are going to survive is altogether different from predicting that we will survive. And describing the steps we will need to take if we want to prevent violence is altogether different from saying that we will take those steps. My purpose in this book is neither to attempt to predict the future, nor to tell other people what they should do; it is simply to summarize what our choices are, and to mention that each of those choices has costs and benefits, so that people can choose what they want with as much knowledge as possible of what they are choosing, what it is likely to cost them, and what they will get in return. I am hoping that some of the lessons I have learned from years of work devoted to preventing violence within the most violent institutions and among the most violent individuals and groups in our society—my laboratory for the study of violence—can prove to be relevant and helpful to us in our attempt to understand what we can do, and will need to do, in order to prevent violence wherever it occurs, on whatever scale and in whatever context—from homicide and suicide to terrorism and race riots to war and genocide. I believe that there are certain causes or motives that are common to all forms of violence, so that there are also certain principles of prevention that are common to all.

I have attempted to write this book not as a philosopher or a moralist, telling people how they *should* live, but as a physician and a natural scientist, describing how we *can* live—that is, which strategies for living (and that means living together, for we are a social species) succeed in sustaining life (that is, preventing violence), and which ones lead to death (by violence). Darwin wrote about the origin of species—all species. I am writing about how to avoid the extinction of a species—our species. I believe that General MacArthur was profoundly correct and far-sighted when he said that the ultimate outcome of modern war, in this era of thermonuclear weapons, was "mutual total annihilation." It is ironic that he of all people should have said that, given that he was the same general whom President Truman had to relieve of his command in Korea because he was unwilling to settle for a limited war, even implying that we should not rule out the use of atomic bombs. Was he motivated to warn us about the dangers of modern weapons because he came so close to using them? Many thinkers have recognized for a long time now that if we do not eliminate war, war will eliminate us. Preventing violence, then, is simply the necessary prerequisite for the survival of our species. It is a project of evolutionary significance.

CHAPTER 1

SHAME AND THE DEATH OF SELF

In the course of my psychotherapeutic work with violent criminals, I was surprised to discover that I kept getting the same answer when I asked one man after another why he had assaulted or even killed someone: "Because he disrespected me." In fact, they used that phrase so often that they abbreviated it to, "He dis'ed me." Whenever people use a word so often that they abbreviate it, you know how central it is in their moral and emotional vocabulary. References to the desire for respect as the motive for violence kept recurring, with remarks like, "I never got so much respect before in my life as I did when I first pointed a gun at some dude's face." On another occasion, I could not understand why one of the prisoners was engaged in a running battle with the prison officers that resulted in his finally being sentenced to solitary confinement and having every privilege and possession taken away from him. I asked him, "What do you want so badly that you are willing to give up everything else in order to get it?"—because it seemed to me that that was exactly what he had done. In response, this man, who was usually so inarticulate that it was difficult to get a clear answer to any question, astonished me by standing up tall, looking me in the eye, and replying with perfect clarity: "Pride. Dignity. Self-esteem." And then he described how the officers were, he felt, attempting to take away his last shred of pride and self-respect by disrespecting him, and said, "If you ain't got pride, you got nothin'."

These experiences, and many others like them, convinced me that the basic psychological motive, or cause, of violent behavior is the wish to ward off or eliminate the feeling of shame and humiliation—a feeling that is painful, and can even be intolerable and overwhelming—and replace it with its opposite, the feeling of pride. I will use these two terms—shame and pride—as generic terms to refer to two whole families of feelings. Synonyms for pride include self-esteem, self-love, self-respect, feelings of self-worth, dignity, and the sense of having maintained one's honor intact. But pride must be in much shorter supply than shame, because there are literally dozens of synonyms for shame, including feelings of being slighted, insulted, disrespected, dishonored, disgraced, disdained, slandered, treated with contempt, ridiculed, teased, taunted, mocked, rejected, defeated, subjected to indignity or ignominy; feelings of inferiority, inadequacy, incompetency; feelings of being weak, ugly, a failure, "losing face," being treated as if you were insignificant, unimportant or worthless, or any of the numerous other forms of what psychoanalysts call "narcissistic injuries." As Franz Alexander wrote in "Some Comments," (1938), the psychology of narcissism is the psychology of shame and its equivalent, feelings of inferiority. Envy and jealousy are members of this same family of feelings: people feel inferior to those whom they envy, or of whom they are jealous. People become *indignant* (and may become violent) when they suffer an *indignity*; language itself reveals the link between shame and rage.

In my previous book, I spoke of shame as the pathogen that causes violence just as specifically as the tubercle bacillus causes tuberculosis, except that in the case of violence it is an emotion, not a microbe—the emotion of shame and humiliation. It is because this emotion is so powerful and pervasive, and so central to the experience of many people, especially those who are predisposed to violence, that there are so many synonyms for it, just as the Japanese and the Chinese have dozens of words for different varieties of silk and silkworms, because of the centrality of these in their culture.

When I first realized what I was hearing from the violent men I was working with, I began to think that I had discovered something original—something previously unknown. Then I happened to reread a passage in the Bible, the story of the first recorded murder in Western history, that I had read many times before without actually understanding what it was saying. It had never been clear to me why Cain killed Abel. But having sat down and talked with people who had actually committed murders, and asking them why, I was at last able to "hear" what the story of Cain and Abel was saying. The Bible makes it very clear why Cain killed Abel: "The Lord had *respect* unto Abel and to his offering: But unto Cain. . .he had *not respect*." In other words, God "dis'ed" Cain. Or rather, Cain was "dis'ed" because of Abel—and he acted out his anger over this insult in exactly the same way as the murderers with whom I was working.

As I read further, I began to realize that this insight has been expressed centuries and even millennia ago, not only in the great myths of our tradition, but also in the writings of the great philosophers and theologians. Both Aristotle (*Rhetoric*, 1378–80) and Aquinas (*Summa Theologica*, I–II Q. 47, II–II Q. 41), for example, stated very clearly that the cause of the desire to assault or injure others is the anger that is caused by feeling that they have been "slighted" by them, and therefore feel justified in getting revenge for the slight. Both of those thinkers make it clear that what they mean by "slighting" is exactly what I am describing here: insulting, ridiculing, disdaining, dishonoring; in short, any behavior that shames people by treating them with contempt and disrespect, as though they are unimportant or insignificant. In other words, the hypothesis regarding the psychological cause or motivation of violence that I thought I had originated has been around in one form or another for a very long time. On the other hand, if it is a valid hypothesis, it would be surprising if earlier thinkers had not also discovered the same thing; for after all, violence has been with us since the dawn of history, and it would be surprising if the greatest minds and the most perceptive observers in history had not also noticed the same regularities in human behavior.

More recent examples would include Hegel, who identified the desire for recognition as the central motive force behind all human history. "Recognition" is a synonym for respect, which means, literally, to be looked back at (re-spectare), or re-cognized, so it is also a synonym for honor, pride, attention, and all other forms of narcissistic gratification. And history itself, as Hegel and many other philosophers of history have noted, is largely the history of violence—wars, assassinations, revolutions, and so on. Although Marx turned Hegel "on his head," as he put it, he agreed with him to the extent of noting that shame is the emotion of revolution (shame being the emotion people feel when they are not recognized, or respected).

The same conclusion as to the psychological cause of violence has also been reached by contemporary scholars from the whole range of the behavioral sciences: clinical psychoanalysis, experimental psychology, social learning theory, sociology, anthropology, criminology, even law-enforcement. The psychoanalyst Heinz Kohut, for example, wrote: "The deepest level to which psychoanalysis can penetrate when it traces destructiveness [is to] the presence of a serious narcissistic injury, an injury that threatened the cohesion of the self."(*The Restoration of the Self,* 1977.) Another analyst, Gregory Rochlin made the same point when he emphasized "the relation of injured narcissism to aggression [and of] humiliation to violence," and concluded, "The question is, what makes people so prone to feeling vulnerable and humiliated, and therefore ultimately what causes violence."(*Man's Aggression,* 1973.) Herbert Thomas in "Experiencing a Shame Response" (1995) schematized the steps leading up to an act of violence as beginning with a rejection, which elicits intensely painful feelings of shame, to which the person responds with anger, which he then expresses or acts out with an act of violence.

Experimental psychologists have reached the same conclusion. Many individual studies and several reviews of the published research literature have been devoted to the study of aggressive behavior and simulated violence elicited under experimental conditions in psychological laboratories. These concern, for example, experiments in which an attempt is made to induce the subject to press a button that he is told will administer painful and potentially injurious or even lethal electrical shocks to another person. The consensus that has emerged from this work is that the most potent stimulus of aggression and violence, and the one that is most reliable in eliciting this response, is not frustration *per se* (as the "frustration-aggression" hypothesis had claimed), but rather, insult and humiliation. In other words, the most effective way, and often the only way, to provoke someone to become violent is to insult him. Feshbach, in "The Dynamics and Morality of Violence and Aggression" (1971), for example, after reviewing the literature on this subject, concluded that "violations to self-esteem through insult, humiliation or coercion are probably the most important source of anger and aggressive drive in humans." (It should be stressed that coercion, as a violation of autonomy, also produces feelings of shame, as Erik Erikson stressed—pride is dependent on being independent.) Geen, in "Effects of Frustration" (1968), concluded that personal insult was more powerful in provoking aggressive behavior than frustration. Sabini, in another review of the literature, generalized:

> Frustration *per se* does not lead to anger. If frustration is not the cause of anger, what is? According to Aristotle, the perception that one has been insulted leads to anger. . . . Curiously, when psychologists have tried to produce anger in the laboratory, even when they have written about their results in terms of the consequences of frustration, they have not relied very much on frustrating people but have much more commonly insulted people—possibly because it is very difficult to make adults angry just by frustrating them.
>
> ("Aggression in the Laboratory," 1978)

The only situation in which frustration without deliberate insult was found to elicit anger was when the frustration was unjustified (e.g. a bus driver deliberately bypassing a bus stop). This does not constitute an exception to the principle that anger and violence are caused by feeling shamed, however, for the perception that one has been a victim of injustice elicits feelings of shame: over being valued so little by the other person, and for being too weak to make him treat one fairly (which is why Marx's insight into the motivation for violent revolution, mentioned above, makes psychological sense). In fact, the Latin word for injustice, *iniuria*, also means "insult" (as well as "injury"). One does not need to add insult to injury, or to injustice; it is already contained within both of those experiences, as it is in the words used to refer to them. The perception that one has been a perpetrator of injustice, by contrast, elicits feelings of guilt.

A number of sociologists have arrived at the same explanation of the psychological roots of human violence. Thomas Scheff and

Suzanne Retzinger, for example, in *Emotions and Violence* (1991) wrote that "a particular sequence of emotions underlies all destructive aggression: shame is first evoked, which leads to rage and then violence." The criminologist David Luckenbill in "Criminal Homicide" (1977) analyzed the step-by-step escalation of the confrontations between victim and perpetrator that led to all seventy murders that occurred in one California county over a ten-year period, 1963–72, and found that in all cases the murderer had interpreted his violence as the only means by which to save or maintain "face", and to demonstrate that his character was strong rather than weak, in a situation that he interpreted as casting doubt on that assessment of himself. The opening move that started this process was some behavior by the victim that the perpetrator interpreted as insulting or disparaging to him and that would cause him to "lose face" if he "backed down" rather than responding with violence—even when the victim was only a child who refused to stop crying when ordered to.

Another sociologist, Elijah Anderson has been conducting ethnographic fieldwork in ghetto areas of Philadelphia for many years, studying the causes of violence currently devastating many urban neighborhoods. He discovered that:

> The street culture has evolved a 'code of the street,' which amounts to
> a set of informal rules of behavior organized around a desperate search
> for respect, that governs public social relations, especially violence. . . .
> At the heart of the code is the issue of respect—loosely defined as being
> treated"right" or being granted one's proper due, or the deference one
> deserves. Respect is viewed as almost an external entity, one that is hard-
> won but easily lost—and so must constantly be guarded. . . . Something
> extremely valuable on the street—respect—is at stake in every interaction.
> . . .For people unfamiliar with the code this concern with respect in the
> most ordinary interactions can be frightening and incomprehensible. . . .
> Many feel that it is acceptable to risk dying over issues of respect. . . .
> There is a general sense that very little respect is to be had, and therefore
> everyone competes to get what affirmation he can from what is available.
> The resulting craving for respect gives people thin skins and short fuses.
>
> *(Code of the Street, 1999)*

All this occurs against the background of life among the ghetto poor, who suffer the absence of jobs that pay a living wage, and the stigma of racial discrimination. He adds that "in a society where so much economic inequality exists, for the severely alienated and desperate a gun can become like a bank card—an equalizer" in the contest for respect, and for the material status symbols that serve as one of the main bases of respect.

Nor is it only behavioral scientists and academicians who have reached these conclusions. The same findings have been reported by law-enforcement officers who have investigated the motives of murderers and other violent criminals. John Douglas was a "profiler" with the F.B.I. whose career was devoted to studying the personalities and attempting to discern the motives of the most violent and dangerous criminals in the United States. What he concluded was that any ultimate violent act "is the result of a deep-seated feeling of inadequacy," and that these men attempt to diminish their low self-esteem by blaming others for their own real or imagined shortcomings, which were often caused, he discovered, by the way they were treated by overly authoritarian fathers (*The Anatomy of Motive*, 1999).

The degree to which a person experiences feelings of shame depends on two variables: the way other people are treating him (with admiration and respect, or with contempt and disdain), and the degree to which he himself already feels proud or ashamed. The more a person is shamed by others, from childhood by parents or peers who ridicule or reject him, the more he is likely to feel chronically shamed, and hypersensitive to feelings and experiences of being shamed, sometimes to the point of feeling that others are treating him with contempt or disdain even when they are not. For such people, and they are the rule among the violent, even a minor sign of real or imagined disrespect can trigger a homicidal reaction.

The purpose of violence is to force respect from other people. The less self-respect people feel, the more they are dependent on respect from others; for without a certain minimal amount of respect, from others or the self, the self begins to feel dead inside, numb and empty. That is how the most violent criminals told me they felt, and it is clear that it is the most intolerable of all feelings (though it is actually an absence of feeling, lack of the feeling of pride, or self-love). When people lack self-respect, and feel they are incapable of eliciting respect from others in the form of admiration for their achievements or their personalities, they may see no way to get respect except in the form of fear, which I think of as a kind of *ersatz* substitute for admiration; and violence does elicit fear, as it is intended to. For example, I have spoken to many violent criminals who spoke of how gratifying it was to see fear in the eyes of their victims.

Feelings of shame and self-contempt are often overlooked by others, because the people who experience them do their best to conceal such feelings behind a defensive mask of bravado and boasting. There is nothing more shameful than to feel ashamed—it reveals that a person has something to feel ashamed about.

Why are these feelings of shame and self-contempt so bottomless, chronic, and almost ineradicable in the most violent men? Because, in the men I knew, they had been subjected to a degree of child abuse that was off the scale of anything I had previously thought of describing with that term. Many had been beaten nearly to death, raped repeatedly or prostituted, or neglected to a life-threatening degree by parents too disabled themselves to care for their child. And of those who had not experienced those extremes of physical abuse or neglect, my colleagues and I found that they had experienced a degree of emotional abuse that had been just as damaging: being focused on as the parents' emotional "whipping boy," in which they served as the scapegoat for whatever feelings of shame and humiliation their parents had suffered and then attempted to rid themselves of by transferring them onto their child, by subjecting him to systematic and chronic shaming and humiliation, taunting and ridicule (Frazier, *Aggression*, 1974).

On the other hand, everyone gets shamed or slighted at one time or another, yet most people never commit a serious act of violence. In that respect, shaming is to violence as the tubercle bacillus is to tuberculosis, a necessary but not a sufficient cause. Even the most violent people are not violent most of the time. Before people will resort to violence, and it is always a last resort, several further preconditions need to be in place. One is that they have not (yet) developed the capacity for the feelings that prevent most of us from behaving violently no matter how much shame, disrespect, dishonor, or insult we are subjected to, such as guilt and remorse over hurting someone else; empathy, love, and concern for others; and even the rational self-interested fear of the retribution that violent behavior provokes from others.

A second precondition that enormously increases the likelihood that people will respond to feelings of shame by means of violence is that they do not perceive themselves as having non-violent means by which to maintain or restore their self-esteem and self-respect. Most of us have such means, such as education, knowledge, skills, and achievements that are honored and respected by others and by ourselves; a profession or career, and some standing or status in the community and with one's family and friends. It is also important not to underestimate the degree to which the self-esteem of many if not most people, in the very materialist, capitalist culture in which we have all been raised and in which we have to live, is dependent on having whatever minimal degree of wealth or income they need in order to feel that their "net worth" (in the accountant's sense) reinforces their sense of "self-worth" (in the psychological sense). The people who become violent criminals, and end up in prison, are notably lacking in all of those non-violent sources of self-esteem: they are overwhelmingly poor, uneducated (many are illiterate), lacking in any skills that they or others could respect, and of the lowest possible social and economic status in society. As the poor, they are lower class; and as members of minority groups (which often means people of color) they are of lower caste (which increases the risk that they will be poor, or lower class, as well). So when they are shamed, they do not have enough non-violent internal or external sources of self-esteem with which to compensate. Violence is their last resort in the literal sense that it is their last resource. And that brings us to another category among the multiple (but related) causes of violence.

CHAPTER 2

THE SOCIAL CAUSES OF VIOLENCE

In order to understand the spread of contagious disease so that one can prevent epidemics, it is just as important to know the vector by which the pathogenic organism that causes the disease is spread throughout the population as it is to identify the pathogen itself. In the nineteenth century, for example, the water supply and the sewer system were discovered to be vectors through which some diseases became epidemic. What is the vector by which shame, the pathogen that causes violence, is spread to its hosts, the people who succumb to the illness of violence?

There is a great deal of evidence, which I will summarize here, that shame is spread via the social and economic system. This happens in two ways. The first is through what we might call the "vertical" division of the population into a hierarchical ranking of upper and lower status groups, chiefly classes, castes, and age groups, but also other means by which people are divided into in-groups and out-groups, the accepted and the rejected, the powerful and the weak, the rich and the poor, the honored and the dishonored. For people are shamed on a systematic, wholesale basis, and their vulnerability to feelings of humiliation is increased when they are assigned an inferior social or economic status; and the more inferior and humble it is, the more frequent and intense the feelings of shame, and the more frequent and intense the acts of violence. The second way is by what we could call the "horizontal" asymmetry of social roles, or gender roles, to which the two sexes are assigned in patriarchal cultures, one consequence of which is that men are shamed or honored for different and in some respects opposite behavior from that which brings shame or honor to women. That is, men are shamed for not being violent enough (called cowards or even shot as deserters), and are more honored the more violent they are (with medals, promotions, titles, and estates)—violence for men is successful as a strategy. Women, however, are shamed for being too active and aggressive (called bitches or unfeminine) and honored for being passive and submissive—violence is much less likely to protect them against shame.

Relative Poverty and Unemployment

The most powerful predictor of the homicide rate in comparisons of the different nations of the world, the different states in the United States, different counties, and different cities and census tracts, is the size of the disparities in income and wealth between the rich and the poor. Some three dozen studies, at least, have found statistically significant correlations between the degree of absolute as well as relative poverty and the incidence of homicide. Hsieh and Pugh in 1993 did a meta-analysis of thirty-four such studies and found strong statistical support for these findings, as have several other reviews of this literature: two on homicide by Smith and Zahn in 1999; Chasin in 1998; Short in 1997; James in 1995; and individual studies, such as Braithwaite in 1979 and Messner in 1980.

On a worldwide basis, the nations with the highest inequities in wealth and income, such as many Third World countries in Latin America, Africa, and Asia, have the highest homicide rates (and also the most collective or political violence). Among the developed nations, the United States has the highest inequities in wealth and income, and also has by far the highest homicide rates, five to ten times larger than the other First World nations, all of which have the lowest levels of inequity and relative poverty in the world, and the lowest homicide rates. Sweden and Japan, for example, have had the lowest degree of inequity in the world in recent years, according to the World Bank's measures; but in fact, all the other countries of western Europe, including Ireland and the United Kingdom, as well as Canada, Australia, and New Zealand, have a much more equal sharing of their collective wealth and income than either the United States or virtually any of the Second or Third World countries, as well as the lowest murder rates.

Those are cross-sectional studies, which analyze the populations being studied at one point in time. Longitudinal studies find the same result: violence rates climb and fall over time as the disparity in income rises and decreases, both in the less violent and the more violent nations. For example, in England and Wales, as Figures 1 and 2 show, there was an almost perfect fit between the rise in several different measures of the size of the gap between the rich and the poor, and the number of serious crimes recorded by the police between 1950 and 1990. Figure 1 shows two measures of the gradual widening of income differences, which accelerated dramatically from 1984 and 1985. Figure 2 shows the increasing percentage of households and families living in relative poverty, a rate that has been particularly rapid since the late 1970s, and also the number of notifiable offences recorded by the police during the same years. As you can see, the increase in crime rates follows the increase in rates of relative poverty almost perfectly. As both inequality and crime accelerated their growth rates simultaneously, the annual *increases* in crime from one year to the next became larger than the *total* crime rate had been in the early 1950s. If we examine the rates for murder alone during the same period, as reported by the Home Office, we find the same pattern, namely a progression from a murder rate that averaged 0.6 per 100,000 between 1946 and 1970, increased to 0.9 from 1971–78, and increased yet again to an average of 1.1 between 1979 and 1997 (with a range of 1.0 to 1.3) To put it another way, 1.2 and 1.3, the five highest levels since the end of World War II, were recorded in 1987, 1991, 1994, 1995 and 1997, all twice as high as the 1946–70 average.

The same correlation between violence and relative poverty has been found in the United States. The economist James Galbraith in *Created Unequal* (1997) has used inequity in wages as one measure of the size and history of income inequity between the rich and the poor from 1920 to 1992. If we correlate this with fluctuations in the American homicide rate during the same period, we find that both wage inequity and the homicide rate increased sharply in the slump of 1920–21, and remained at those historically high levels until the Great Crash of 1929, when they both jumped again, literally doubling

Figure 1   Increasing Income Differences U.K. 1979–99

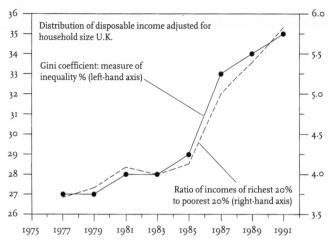

The Gini coefficient, the solid line, measures inequality, not just between rich and poor, but among the whole population. It can vary between 0%, meaning everyone had the same income, to 100%, meaning that one person had all the income. The dotted line records the growing disparity between the richest and poorest 20% of the population. (After Figure 1 in Richard G. Wilkinson, *Unfair Shares*, Barnardo's, 1994.)

Figure 2   Relative Poverty and Serious Crime England and Wales 1950–91

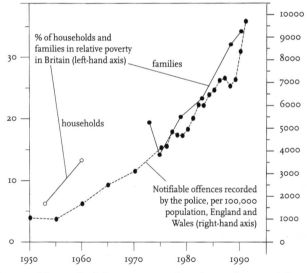

The solid lines record the growth of relative poverty (% of population with incomes below 50% of the median income, allowing for the number of people in each household or family) since 1953. There was a dramatic rise in the proportion in relative poverty in Britain after the late 1970s, and also a sharp rise in serious crime in England and Wales, shown by the dotted line. (After Figures 13 and 14 in Richard G. Wilkinson, *Unfair Shares*, Barnardo's, 1994.)

together and suddenly, to the highest levels ever observed up to that time. These record levels of economic inequality (which increase, as Galbraith shows, when unemployment increases) were accompanied by epidemic violence; both murder rates and wage inequity remained twice as high as they had previously been, until the economic leveling effects of Roosevelt's New Deal, beginning in 1933, and the Second World War a few years later, combined to bring both violence and wage inequity down by the end of the war to the same low levels as at the end of the First World War, and they both remained at those low levels for the next quarter of a century, from roughly 1944 to 1968.

That was the modern turning point. In 1968 the median wage began falling, after having risen steadily for the previous three decades, and "beginning in 1969 inequality started to rise, and continued to increase sharply for fifteen years," (J. K. Galbraith). The homicide rate soon reached levels *twice* as high as they had been during the previous quarter of a century (1942–66). Both wage inequality and homicide rates remained at those relatively high levels for the next quarter of a century, from 1973 to 1997. That is, the murder rate averaged 5 per 100,000 population from 1942 to 1966, and 10 per 100,000 from 1970 to 1997. Finally, by 1998 unemployment dropped to the lowest level since 1970; both the minimum wage and the median wage began increasing again in real terms for the first time in thirty years; and the poverty rate began dropping. Not surprisingly, the homicide rate also fell, for the first time in nearly thirty years, below the range in which it had been fluctuating since 1970–71 (though both rates, of murder and of economic inequality, are still higher than they were from the early 1940s to the mid-1960s).

As mentioned before, unemployment rates are also relevant to rates of violence. M. H. Brenner found that every one per cent rise in the unemployment rate is followed within a year by a 6 per cent rise in the homicide rate, together with similar increases in the rates of suicide, imprisonment, mental hospitalization, infant mortality, and deaths from natural causes such as heart attacks and strokes (*Mental Illness and the Economy*, 1973, and "Personal Stability and Economic Security," 1977). Theodore Chiricos reviewed sixty-three American studies and concluded that while the relationship between unemployment and crime may have been inconsistent during the 1960s (some studies found a relationship, some did not), it became overwhelmingly positive in the 1970s, as unemployment changed from a brief interval between jobs to enduring worklessness ("Rates of Crime and Unemployment," 1987). David Dickinson found an exceptionally close relationship between rates of burglary and unemployment for men under twenty-five in the U.K. in the 1980s and 1990s ("Crime and Unemployment," 1993). Bernstein and Houston have also found statistically significant correlations between unemployment and crime rates, and negative correlations between wages and crime rates, in the U.S. between 1989 and 1998 (*Crime and Work*, 2000).

If we compare Galbraith's data with U.S. homicide statistics, we find that the U.S. unemployment rate has moved in the same direction as the homicide rate from 1920 to 1992: increasing sharply in 1920–21, then jumping to even higher levels from the Crash of 1929 until Roosevelt's reforms began in 1933, at which point the rates of both unemployment and homicide also began to fall, a trend that accelerated further with the advent of the war. Both rates then remained low (with brief fluctuations) until 1968, when they began a steady rise which kept them both at levels higher than they had been in any postwar period, until the last half of 1997, when unemployment fell below that range and has continued to decline ever since, followed closely by the murder rate.

Why do economic inequality and unemployment both stimulate violence? Ultimately, because both increase feelings of shame (Gilligan, *Violence*). For example, we speak of the poor as the lower classes, who have lower social and economic status, and the rich as the upper classes who have higher status. But the Latin for lower is *inferior*, and the word for the lower classes in Roman law was the *humiliores*. Even in English, the poor are sometimes referred to as the humbler classes. Our language itself tells us that to be poor is to be humiliated and inferior, which makes it more difficult not to feel inferior. The word for upper or higher was *superior*, which is related to the word for pride, *superbia* (the opposite of shame), also the root of our word superb (another antonym of inferior). And a word for the upper classes, in Roman law, was the *honestiores* (related to the word honor, also the opposite of shame and dishonor).

Inferiority and superiority are relative concepts, which is why it is relative poverty, not absolute poverty, that exposes people to feelings of inferiority. When everyone is on the same level, there is no shame in being poor, for in those circumstances the very concept of poverty loses its meaning. Shame is also a function of the gap between one's level of aspiration and one's level of achievement. In a society with extremely rigid caste or class hierarchies, it may not feel so shameful to be poor, since it is a matter of bad luck rather than of any personal failing. Under those conditions, lower social status may be more likely to motivate apathy, fatalism, and passivity (or "passive aggressive-ness"), and to inhibit ambition and the need for achievement, as Gunnar Myrdal noted in many of the caste-ridden peasant cultures that he studied in *Asian Drama* (1968). Caste-ridden cultures, however, may have the potential to erupt into violence on a revolution-ary or even genocidal scale, once they reject the notion that the caste or class one is born into is immutable, and replace it with the notion that one has only oneself to blame if one remains poor while others are rich. This we have seen repeatedly in the political and revolutionary violence that has characterized the history of Indonesia, Kampuchea, India, Ceylon, China, Vietnam, the Philippines, and many other areas throughout Asia during the past half-century.

All of which is another way of saying that one of the costs people pay for the benefits associated with belief in the "American Dream," the myth of equal opportunity, is an increased potential for violence. In fact, the social and economic system of the United States combines almost every characteristic that maximizes shame and hence violence. First, there is the "Horatio Alger" myth that everyone can get rich if they are smart and work hard (which means that if they are not rich they must be stupid or lazy, or both). Second, we are not only told that we can get rich, we are also stimulated to want to get rich. For the whole economic system of mass production depends on whetting people's appetites to consume the flood of goods that are being produced (hence the flood of advertisements). Third, the social and economic reality is the opposite of the Horatio Alger myth, since social mobility is actually less likely in the U.S. than in the supposedly more rigid social structures of Europe and the U.K. As Mishel, Bernstein and Schmitt have noted:

> Contrary to widely held perceptions, the U.S. offers less economic mobility than other rich countries. In one study, for example, low-wage workers in the U.S. were more likely to remain in the low-wage labor market five years longer than workers in Germany, France, Italy, the United Kingdom, Denmark, Finland, and Sweden (all the other countries studied in this analysis). In another study, poor households in the U.S. were less likely to leave poverty from one year to the next than were poor households in Canada, Germany, the Netherlands, Sweden, and the United Kingdom (all the countries included in this second analysis).
>
> (*The State of Working America 2000–2001*, 2001)

Fourth, as they also mention, "the U.S. has the most unequal income distribution and the highest poverty rates among all the advanced economies in the world. The U.S. tax and benefit system is also one of the least effective in reducing poverty." The net effect of all these features of U.S society is to maximize the gap between aspiration and attainment, which maximizes the frequency and intensity of feelings of shame, which maximizes the rates of violent crimes.

It is difficult not to feel inferior if one is poor when others are rich, especially in a society that equates self-worth with net worth; and it is difficult not to feel rejected and worthless if one cannot get or hold a job while others continue to be employed. Of course, most people who lose jobs or income do not commit murders as a result; but there are always some men who are just barely maintaining their self-esteem at minimally tolerable levels even when they do have jobs and incomes. And when large numbers of them lose those sources of self-esteem, the number who explode into homicidal rage increases as measurably, regularly, and predictably as any epidemic does when the balance between pathogenic forces and the immune system is altered.

And those are not just statistics. I have seen many individual men who have responded in exactly that way under exactly these circumstances. For example, one African-American man was sent to the prison mental hospital I directed in order to have a psychiatric evaluation before his murder trial. A few months before that, he had had a good job. Then he was laid off at work, but he was so ashamed of this that he concealed the fact from his wife (who was a schoolteacher) and their children, going off as if to work every morning and returning at the usual time every night. Finally, after two or three months of this, his wife noticed that he was not bringing in any money. He had to admit the truth, and then his wife fatally said, "What kind of man are you? What kind of man would behave this way?" To prove that he was a man, and to undo the feeling of emasculation, he took out his gun and shot his wife and children. (Keeping a gun is, of course, also a way that some people reassure themselves that they are really men.) What I was struck by, in addition to the tragedy of the whole story, was the intensity of the shame he felt over being unemployed, which led him to go to such lengths to conceal what had happened to him.

Caste Stratification

Caste stratification also stimulates violence, for the same reasons. The United States, perhaps even more than the other Western democracies, has a caste system that is just as real as that of India, except that it is based on skin color and ethnicity more than on hereditary occupation. The fact that it is a caste system similar to India's is registered by the fact that in my home city, Boston, members of the highest caste are called "Boston Brahmins" (a.k.a. "WASPs," or White Anglo-Saxon Protestants). The lowest rung on the caste ladder, corresponding to the "untouchables" or Harijan, of India, is occupied by African-Americans, Native Americans, and some Hispanic-Americans. To be lower caste is to be rejected, socially and vocationally, by the upper castes, and regarded and treated as inferior. For example, whites often move out of neighborhoods when blacks move in; blacks are "the last to be hired and the first to be fired," so that their unemployment rate has remained twice as high as the white rate ever since it began being measured; black citizens are arrested and publicly humiliated under circumstances in which no white citizen would be; respectable white authors continue to write books and articles claiming that blacks are intellectually inferior to whites; and so on and on, *ad infinitum*. It is not surprising that the constant shaming and attributions of inferiority to which the lower caste groups are subjected would cause members of those groups to feel shamed, insulted, disrespected, disdained, and treated as inferior—because they have been, and because many of their greatest writers and leaders have told us that this is how they feel they have been treated by whites. Nor is it surprising that this in turn would give rise to feelings of resentment if not rage, nor that the most vulnerable, those who lacked any non-violent means of restoring their sense of personal dignity, such as educational achievements, success, and social status, might well see violence as the only way of expressing those feelings. And since one of the major disadvantages of lower-caste status is lack of equal access to educational and vocational opportunities, it is not surprising that the rates of homicide and other violent crimes among all the lower-caste groups mentioned are many times higher, year after year, than those of the upper-caste groups.

Age Discrimination

Age discrimination has the same effect, particularly for young males. Throughout the world, the most concrete sources of pride, such as power, wealth, status, and honorific titles and positions, are disproportionately given to older males, and denied to younger ones. That is, in virtually every social system in which there are military, religious, governmental, financial, or educational status hierarchies, the higher-status positions are disproportionately awarded to those who are older. Sometimes this is even required by law. In the United States, for example, one has to be twenty-five to become a Congressman, thirty to become a Senator, and thirty-five to become President. The lowest incomes are paid to those who are just beginning their careers, whereas the highest are found among those who are older. Of all age groups in the U.S., the highest rates of poverty are found among those under the age of eighteen, and unemployment rates are higher for young males than for older and middle-aged ones, year after year. In fact, ever since the values of Western culture were first codified at the dawn of history, in the Ten Commandments, the elderly have been accorded more honor than the young—"Thou shalt honour thy father and mother"—with not a word about honouring the son or daughter.

But the young are not only given less access to the sources of honor and pride, they are also disproportionately subjected to the sources of shame and humiliation. For example, until only a few years ago the legal systems of every nation permitted adults (parents, baby-sitters, teachers, etc.) to engage in the corporal punishment of children, behavior that would constitute assault and battery if committed on another adult, such as slapping and hitting, including with sticks, rulers, belts, and other objects. Even today, only ten nations forbid all corporal punishment, even by parents (the Scandinavian countries, Latvia, Croatia, Austria, Italy, Israel, and Cyprus), and only one state in the U.S., Minnesota (where many are of Scandinavian descent). Although the United Kingdom is less permissive of this practice than is the U.S., in that it forbids teachers from hitting children, it still permits parents to do so. We know that assaults of this sort are experienced by children as humiliating, because they tell us so, both at the time and in later years. Indeed, the adults who behave in this way are usually quite clear that their aim is to "humble" the child, and they succeed all too well (though the effect is to teach the child to "humble" others by assaulting them as well). Etymology also teaches us that an assault is experienced emotionally as an insult: the two words come from the same Latin root, and even in English they have overlapping meanings. So even when it does not produce physical injury, the corporal punishment of children conveys a clear symbolic message that children are inferior to adults and are not to be treated with respect, and that it is permissible to hit someone if you happen to be stronger than they are.

But the singling out of the young for legally permitted degrees of violence and humiliation does not end with childhood; it continues and even intensifies after they reach puberty and young adulthood. For only the young, throughout history and in every nation on earth, have been forced to fight each other, killing and being killed, in the wars that are declared by the middle-aged and elderly, wars in which they themselves are exempt from the obligation to risk their lives by engaging in front-line combat. The old saying that war is the revenge of the old on the young captures a deep psychological truth, one that is reflected in the revenge that the young adults themselves then take, first by committing most of the murders and rapes that are recorded, and then, after they reach middle age themselves, by inflicting the same violence on the young that was inflicted on them, whether as parents assaulting their own children or as political and military leaders sending the young to their deaths, in the endless vicious circle (and in this instance it really is vicious) of violence that repeats from one generation to the next.

My point here is not to argue that there are never rational reasons for differentiating in law and custom between the rights and responsibilities that are accorded to people of different ages. The younger children are, the more helpless and dependent they are, and it would also be a form of child abuse not to recognize those differences. But it is one thing to distinguish between real differences in needs and abilities, and another to single out one group for disproportionate honor and deference, and another for disproportionate shaming and humiliation. My point here is simply to demonstrate how high is the price we pay any time we give respect to one group and deny it to another. One consequence of the way the old treat the young is that the highest rates of violent behavior occur among young males, from when they first attain adult size and strength during adolescence until they reach the age at which they finally begin to accumulate some of the signs of status, which usually occurs around the beginning of middle age (forty years or older). That age group alone—fourteen to thirty-nine—commits more than 90 per cent of the murders, assaults and rapes in the world, and almost all of the military and political violence as well.

Shame Cultures versus Guilt Cultures

The frequency and types of violence vary enormously from one culture to another. Can we identify any characteristics that determine these differences? There is a great deal of evidence that the cultures whose members commit the most violence against others are those whose value systems, socialization practices and major institutions have the effect of making their members especially sensitive and vulnerable to feelings of shame and humiliation; expose them to situations that evoke those feelings; and do not facilitate their developing the kinds of feelings that tend to inhibit violent impulses, such as feelings of guilt and remorse in response to harming others. Conversely, there is also much evidence that cultures that do the opposite have the least inter-personal and collective violence, but may suffer from the opposite problem: excessive feelings of guilt, sin, and responsibility, with a vulnerability to depression, masochism, martyrdom, and suicide (i.e. violence toward the self).

This categorization of cultures derives from Ruth Benedict's concept of shame cultures and guilt cultures, which she introduced in the study of Japanese culture and personality that she prepared during the Second World War, *The Chrysanthemum and the Sword* (1946). As I will use these terms, I do not mean to imply that this difference between cultures is an "either/or" dichotomization; rather, it occurs along at least two major polarities. First, we can differentiate between those that are more or less "pure" shame or guilt cultures, to the degree that they emphasize only one or the other emotion in their socialization practices and moral value systems, versus those that are "mixed," emphasizing both emotions; and between "extreme" versus "mild" shame or guilt cultures, depending on the intensity and frequency of the shame or guilt to which their members are exposed. An example of a relatively pure and extreme shame culture would be the Kwakiutl Indians of Vancouver Island, as described by Ruth Benedict (*Patterns of Culture*, 1934):

> The ultimate reason why a man of the [Kwakiutl] cared about the nobility titles, the wealth. . .and the prerogatives lays bare the mainspring of their culture: they used them in a contest in which they sought to shame their rivals. . . . The object of all Kwakiutl enterprise was to show oneself superior to one's rivals. This will to superiority was carried out with

uncensored self-glorification and with gibes and insults poured upon
the opponents. . . . The Kwakiutl stressed equally the fear of ridicule, and
the interpretation of experience in terms of insults. They recognized only
one gamut of emotion, that which swings between victory and shame.

That this cultural pattern was associated with violence can be seen
from the fact that the Kwakiutl engaged in headhunting, cannibalism,
burning slaves alive, and undiscriminating, merciless war and
murder, even against totally innocent, unsuspecting, hospitable,
sleeping friends, neighbors, relatives, or hosts—men, women, and
children. They would "vie with each other in committing atrocities," as
Ruth Benedict's mentor and the first ethnographer of the Kwakiutl,
Franz Boas, pointed out (*General Anthropology*, 1938). The motive for
this aggressiveness was the desire to wipe out feelings of shame and to
maximize feelings of pride and social prestige; aggressive behavior
was an accepted and honored way of doing this, as Helen Codere also
recognized (*Fighting With Property*, 1950).

A shame culture is one in which the source of moral sanctions and
authority is perceived to reside in other people, in their ridicule,
criticism, or contempt (so that one is shamed in other people's eyes).
The feeling of shame actually occurs in oneself, of course, and can
occur when one is alone, but it is characteristically perceived as something that occurs before an audience, an external judge in whose eyes
(and by comparison with whom) one appears weak, failed, foolish,
incompetent, ridiculous, rejected, inferior, contemptible—in short,
shameful. Thus, shame motivates concealment of those traits in
oneself of which one is ashamed, since shame is only intensified by
exposure to others. A guilt culture is one in which the source of moral
sanctions and authority is oneself, one's own internalized conscience
and the moral law one imposes on oneself, violation of which leaves
one feeling guilty and sinful in one's own eyes. By contrast with
shame, the feeling of guilt or sin is actually relieved by exposure,
which is why guilt cultures institutionalize the practice of confession
of sins. This is understandable, since the person who feels guilty per-
ceives his sin (evil) as being "inside" himself, so to speak, so letting it

"out" through confession can feel like draining a moral abscess, bringing a relief of painful pressure.

But why would the perceived source of moral sanctions and disapproval affect either the likelihood or the direction of violent impulses? The answer, I believe, is that what the feeling of shame motivates most directly is the wish to eliminate the feeling of shame, since it is a very painful feeling; and since shame is seen as emanating from other people, that can be done most directly by eliminating other people. It is true that one could also eliminate the feeling of shame, at lower cost to oneself and others, by means of achievements of which one could feel proud, and which would elicit approval, admiration, respect and honors from others. But that is not always possible, and when it is not, eliminating others may be seen as the only alternative. What the feeling of guilt motivates, correspondingly, is the wish to eliminate the feeling of guilt, since it is a very painful feeling; and since the feeling of guilt emanates from the self, the only way to eliminate it may be by eliminating the self (as in suicide, or by provoking or passively submitting to martyrdom).

Another way to understand why shame motivates anger and violence toward others, and why guilt directs those same feelings and behaviors toward the self, is to remember that in a shame ethic the worst evil is shame, the source of which is perceived as other people (the audience in whose "evil eyes" one is shamed). Therefore evil resides in other people, and to the degree that one feels shame, it is other people who deserve punishment. Punishing others alleviates feelings of shame because it replaces the image of oneself as a weak, passive, helpless, and therefore shameful victim of their punishment (i.e. their shaming) with the contrasting image of oneself as powerful, active, self-reliant, and therefore admirable, and unshameable. In a guilt ethic, by contrast, the worst evil is to be guilty or sinful, and guilt and sin (to the degree that one feels guilty and sinful) are perceived as residing within oneself. Thus, people who feel guilty see themselves as deserving punishment. And receiving punishment, whether from oneself or from others, relieves guilt by expiating it. Indeed, that is the purpose of punishment, both in the criminal law (in which punishment is the means by which the criminal "pays his debt" to society and thus discharges his guilt) and in the religious sacrament of penance (the self-punishment by which the sinner expiates his sins, that is, relieves his guilt-feelings). Thus, *whereas punishment intensifies feelings of shame, it relieves feelings of guilt,* a psychological fact that has important implications for the effect that punishment has on the level of violent crime in a society, as I will discuss further in Chapter 6.

To feel shamed is to perceive oneself as being disrespected, and the most direct and rapid way to make others respect you is to make them afraid of you. This is, of course, an *ersatz* and costly form of respect which people have no need of when they receive genuine respect from others, or when their feelings of self-respect are strong enough to maintain their self-esteem independent of respect from others.

The feeling of shame is also the feeling of being ridiculed, or of being vulnerable to ridicule; and the most direct and certain way to stop people from laughing at you is to make them cry instead. In Shakespeare's *Henry V* the French Dauphin ridicules Henry by making him a gift not of royal treasure but of tennis balls, to which Henry responds by threatening such violence against the French that "thousands shall weep more than did laugh at it." This same principle still causes wars, as well as the kinds of violence that the legal system labels as criminal. Hitler, for example, was elected to power on the basis of the campaign promise to "undo the shame of Versailles." Violence occurs when people see no means of undoing or preventing their own humiliation except by humiliating others; indeed, that is the underlying purpose of inflicting violence on others.

That the values and socialization practices of pure and extreme shame cultures lead to violence is well documented by the cross-cultural data in the Human Relations Area Files (Textor, *A Cross-Cultural Summary,* 1967), a quantified, computerized summary of the past century of research in cultural anthropology, in which several measures of shame show highly significant correlations with several indices of violence. The measures of shame included cultural traits such as extreme "boastfulness," "sensitivity to insult," "invidious display of wealth," and a "composite narcissism index," which is the summation of those and other indices. The cultures that scored high on those indices were significantly more likely than those with low scores to have a high incidence of warfare, bellicosity, killing, torture and mutilation of enemies, pursuit of military glory, crimes against the person (i.e. violent crimes), slavery, alcoholic aggression, male genital mutilation, and so on.

Since pure and extreme guilt cultures tend to prevent rather than cause violence toward others, I will discuss them in Chapter 5 (see the Hutterites). Here it is relevant to note that significant correlations exist in the Human Relations Area Files data not only between the different indices of shame and of violence, but also between both of those variables and several different measures of social and economic inequality. Cultures that have social classes, those that have caste systems, and those that practice slavery, all show significantly more of both shame and violence than cultures whose institutions do not divide people in those hierarchical ways. The existence of inequality exposes everyone to the risk of being inferior, which in turn stimulates aggressive competition to inflict the inferior status on others (such as by enslaving, impoverishing, or degrading them). In other words, inequality stimulates shame and shame stimulates the creation of inequality; shame stimulates violence and violence stimulates shame; inequality leads to violence and violence leads to inequality. These are all mutually reinforcing "vicious circles," or positive-feedback loops.

War and Democracy

One of the most remarkable findings of recent scholarship in political science is that "during the past century there have been no wars between well established democracies" (Weart, *Never At War*, 1998). In the modern world wars have only occurred when at least one of the combatants has been ruled by a dictatorship, oligarchy, or some other non-democratic form of government. Professor Jack Levy ("Domestic Politics and War," 1989) has written that "this absence of war between democracies comes as close as anything we have to an empirical law in international relations." This thesis, if it survives further empirical testing and theoretical analysis, of course has important implications for the prevention of war, which is why I will return to it in the next chapter; but it also implies that a cause of war is an authoritarian political structure, in which there is a high degree of inequality of power.

Naturally, there is much room for debate about such a sweeping generalization, especially over definitions of democracy and of war, and over the theoretical understanding of why the correlation between democracy and peace exists. But the hypothesis seems to me to be plausible enough to pursue further, since it accords with the repeated and remarkably consistent findings in a variety of contexts that violence is associated, to a statistically significant degree, with higher degrees of inequity and hierarchy in the status systems of the social groups being studied, and becomes less frequent and intense the greater the degree of equality.

Even authoritarian individuals are more violent than those whose values are more democratic and egalitarian, as shown in Adorno, et al. in *The Authoritarian Personality* (1950) and Altemeyer in *The Authoritarian Specter* (1996); in fact, the highest scorers in Adorno's study of authoritarianism, or "potential fascism," were violent criminals in San Quentin. The only "neo-Nazis" I myself have ever encountered anywhere have been violent inmates in the maximum security prison, and violent patients in the prison mental hospital. The Adorno study, referring to Ruth Benedict's contrast between shame and guilt cultures, also found that authoritarian personalities were notably sensitive to feelings of shame and insensitive to guilt feelings.

What is true of governments and individuals also seems to be true of families. As Murray Straus and his colleagues have found in their 1980 and 1986 studies of violence in the family, domestic violence is less common the greater the degree to which power and decision-making are shared equally by both spouses. Perhaps relations between nations, despite their greater complexity, do not follow totally different laws. That is, the values that lead people to create authoritarian (inegalitarian) power structures also lead them to be aggressive toward others, and it may only take one such party to a relationship to bring about a violent conflict.

CHAPTER 3

VIOLENCE AS PROOF OF MASCULINITY

If being treated as inferior, or assigned an inferior position in a status hierarchy, leads to feelings of inferiority (shame), and that in turn leads to rage and violence, then why are women not more violent than men? Haven't women been treated as inferior by men ever since the invention of patriarchy? Yet men commit much more violence than women do—homicides, suicides, wars, executions, even the so-called "unintentional" violence that results from careless risk-taking.

Understanding why men are more violent than women requires an understanding of the highly asymmetrical gender roles to which the members of each sex are assigned at birth in our patriarchal culture, and to which they are powerfully conditioned to conform throughout the rest of their lives by virtually all the institutions of our society. The relevant point here is that the differences in those gender roles make it possible for men to ward off or undo feelings of shame, disgrace and dishonor by means of violence, whereas that is significantly less true for women. Masculinity, in the traditional, conventional stereotypical sex-role of patriarchy, is literally defined as involving the expectation, even the requirement, of violence, under many well specified conditions: in time of war; in response to personal insult; in response to extramarital sex on the part of a female in the family; while engaging in all-male combat sports; etc. The Greek term for masculinity, *andreia* (the root of our word androgen), also means "courage." The same is true of the Latin word for manliness and manhood, *virtus*, which also means bravery and courage. The word *virtus* itself derives from *vir*, which means both "man" and "soldier" *(i.e. to be a man is to be a soldier)*. *Virtus* is also the word from which our word "virtue" derives. In the war-like culture of ancient Rome, the original and primary meaning of virtue *was* "courage," the indispensable master virtue for soldiers. In other words, the primary meaning of virtue = courage = manliness = soldier was the willingness to risk one's own life in violent combat with other men. The result of that is that men can prove their manliness, their masculine sexual adequacy, when it has been called into question by an insult or a sign of disrespect, by means of violence; and their failure or unwillingness to engage in violence can throw their manliness into doubt, and expose them to shame.

A Woman's Honor

How are things different for women? In order to discover the decisive difference between male and female gender roles, and how they lead to differing rates of violent behavior, it will be helpful to ask: what circumstances will augment or diminish shame (or honor) for a man, and are those the same as or different from the ones that will have that effect for a woman? And since I am a man I thought it might be especially helpful to consult a woman. Virginia Woolf went some distance toward answering this question in *Three Guineas* (1938), her powerful polemic against patriarchy and male violence. She wrote: "External observation would suggest that a man still feels it a peculiar insult to be taunted with *cowardice* by a woman in much the same way that a woman feels it a peculiar insult to be taunted with *unchastity* by a man." For example, if we ask what are the worst (i.e. most shaming) insults that can be hurled at a man or a woman, respectively, what are they? My own "external observation" (of violent criminals in prisons, among other men over the years) would suggest that for men the insults that are most powerfully shaming, and hence violence-provoking, are those that call into question either their courage or their manliness (two psychologically and etymologically synonymous concepts). These include "wimp," "coward," "sissy," and anything that throws doubt on one's status as a normal, potent, sexually adequate, adult heterosexual male, such as "weirdo," "faggot," or "fairy" (the homophobic insult); "boy" (the traditional insult given to adult black men in American South and South Africa); or the declaration that a man is effeminate or castrated and "has no balls," or that he is a "cuckold," which can be translated into patriarchese as "not enough of a man to control his wife's sexuality." It is important to note that "cuckold" is a term applied exclusively to men, and there is no corresponding word for the woman whose husband is unfaithful to her.

I am not saying that those are the only insults that are so powerfully shaming that they constitute what the legal system has called "fighting words," but that they are the insults that throw the most light on the differential social psychology of men and women. There are also racial insults, for example, which can be equally violence-provoking; but they are equally insulting to both sexes, and are not specifically relevant to the differences between men and women.

For women the situation is entirely different. As Virginia Woolf suggested, women are insulted not by having their courage or their capacity for sexual activity called into question, but rather, by accusations that they are too active sexually, or active outside the bounds their gender role prescribes for them (meaning exclusively in marriage): "slut," "whore," "bitch," "tramp." Just as "cuckold" is applied exclusively to men, "promiscuous" is applied almost exclusively to women. But what is most relevant here is that women are shamed not for being too submissive, dependent, unaggressive, and sexually inactive or impotent, as men are, but rather, for exactly the opposite traits: being too rebellious, independent, aggressive, and sexually active. Thus, if a woman responds to being shamed by becoming aggressive or violent, that may only lead to more shame rather than, as for men, to less— violence on the part of women is regarded, according to patriarchal values, as "unfeminine."

Only men, for example, are expected (and either permitted or forced) to fight in wars (a convention that has only recently begun to be questioned). Even Lady Macbeth, when she was trying to talk herself into becoming violent, prayed to the gods of destruction to "unsex me," for no woman could commit murder! And even then, she could only commit the murder vicariously, using her husband as the instrument of her will, by shaming him, and telling him he would be like a woman if he were too cowardly to kill Duncan.

I am not saying that no woman will respond by resorting to violence; another great tragic heroine, Medea, shows how violent a woman can become when her husband shames her by an infatuation with another woman. I encountered a similar tragedy in reality in the Massachusetts prisons. A woman whose husband had decided to leave her for another woman killed their two children and eventually (unlike Medea) killed herself as well. What I am saying, rather, is that violence is not a ready-made, gender-specific means of undoing shame for women as it is for men; it simply does not work as well. If one shames a woman enough, as Medea was, or as many women of color are shamed in the United States, one can elicit violence in a woman that can be just as homicidal as the violence of a man.

The central implication of all this is that in patriarchal societies men are assigned the role of "violence-objects," and women are assigned the role of "sex-objects." That is, men and only men are assigned the role of fighting in wars, and they are not given any choice about the matter; if they refuse to treat other men as objects of violence, and thereby simultaneously become objects of those men's violence, they will be shamed and insulted (called cowards) and then turned into objects of their own army's violence. "Deserters" have traditionally been shot. And just as men are shamed for refusing to treat other men and themselves as violence-objects, they are honored for being willing to do so. George Bernard Shaw said that if a man steals a hundred pounds he is sent to jail, but if he steals a million pounds he is sent to Parliament. I believe the same principle applies to male violence. If a man kills one person, he is sent to prison; if he kills ten, to a prison mental hospital; but if he is responsible for the death of thousands, he is crowned emperor, made the Duke of Marlborough, or elected President of the United States. The opposite of shame is honor; and the highest honor given by the United States is the Congressional Medal of Honor. Who is it given to? Men. And for what? For violence, or more precisely, for turning themselves and other men into objects of each other's violence. I do not say this in order to shame those who sacrificed their own safety or even their own lives in the attempt to save their comrades-in-arms (and the rest of us) from the violence of other men. I am mentioning these facts in order to clarify the causes of male violence, and to clarify why most lethal violence is committed by males against males, so that we can improve our ability to prevent all violence. My point here is to show why violence can be for men a very powerful way to ward off shame, and to achieve pride and honor instead, whereas it does not serve that purpose for women nearly as frequently or effectively.

What women are honored for, under conditions of patriarchy, is not violence, but sexual chastity outside marriage, and fidelity (and fertility) within marriage. I am calling that female gender role the equivalent of being a "sex-object" because it means that the woman is obliged to renounce her own sexual subjectivity; she is not permitted to have sexual wishes and activities of her own choosing, before, during, or (in some cultures) even after marriage, but must instead be her husband's sex-object. A woman in most patriarchal circum-Mediterranean shame-and-honor cultures will typically be honored for being a virgin until marriage, and shamed if she is not. From this comes the tradition in some peasant cultures of hanging bloody sheets outdoors the morning after the newlyweds' first night together, as a means of proving that neither the family's nor the new husband's honor has been destroyed by unchastity in the bride. By contrast, a man in such cultures may be shamed for being a virgin at marriage, so at puberty he is traditionally taken by his father or older brother to a house of prostitution, or introduced to a mistress.

The fact that both women and men assign themselves and other women and men to the gender roles I have just described (to the extent that they have internalized the values of patriarchy), and that both women and men enforce their conformity to those roles, can be seen by examining the epidemiology of violent crime. In the developed nations, at least, both women and men assign men to the role of violence-objects, for both women and men are more likely to kill a man than they are to kill a woman. That is, both sexes see it as more "appropriate" to kill a man than to kill a woman. The only part of the world in which that might not be true, as a statistical generalization, is in certain Asian societies such as India and China, where lethal violence toward females such as bride-burning and female infanticide, are apparently all too common. I do not know how accurate the statistics are in those developing nations, but there is a discrepancy between reported death rates, in which men are in the majority as they are throughout the rest of the world, and overall census figures, in which men are also reported to outnumber women, which is not true anywhere else in the world.

Another exception: in the most traditional patriarchal societies, women who are perceived as having "dishonoured" the men in their family by engaging in premarital or extramarital sex may be killed by a male relative. And even in less rigidly patriarchal societies, such as the U.K. and the U.S., marital infidelity on the part of the wife is one of the more frequent precipitants of wife-murder. But those exceptions only prove the rule, I think, about the nature of gender roles, for the woman who renounces her assigned gender-role (which is to be the sex-object of her husband) and allows herself to have some sexual subjectivity of her own, thereby also renounces the protection her assigned gender-role gave her from violence.

The statistics on sexual violence show the opposite pattern. There it is very clear that women are seen as sex-objects, for the vast majority of victims of rape are women (a gender disparity that also applies to incest). In fact, being a rape victim is perhaps the most extreme example of what it means to be a sex-object; by definition, the subjective wishes and will of the rape victim are ignored by the rapist. My point here is to distinguish between two types of violence, physical and sexual, in the same way that child abuse is differentiated into physical abuse (the battered-child syndrome, infanticide) and sexual abuse (incest, pedophilia). Both are forms of violence, of course, but they show important differences in their epidemiology and their consequences, which I believe can throw light on the psychology both of gender roles and of violence. I have used the terms violence-object and sex-object for the sake of brevity, but that of course does not mean that rape is not a violent crime. Physical violence can be defined as the inflicting of physical injury or death, and sexual violence as the violation of a person's sexual autonomy.

When men are raped by other men (as many are in prisons), the overt, conscious symbolic meaning of the event is that they are being "turned into women." For example, in prisons in the Southern U.S., a male inmate who has been raped is called a "gal-boy." To be a sex-object *is* to be a woman, and vice versa, in the culture of violence called patriarchy.

A form of violence towards men and women that may superficially appear to be more or less identical, namely genital mutilation, in fact also exemplifies and confirms this same gender-role differentiation. The purpose of mutilating a girl's genitals is to render her sexually anesthetized and inactive, so as to facilitate the task of turning her into a sex-object who will be a virgin before marriage and monogamous after marriage. This is done by removing the basis of her sexual subjectivity, her capacity to have sexual desires and activities of her own, by removing her clitoris and sewing her labia shut. The purpose of mutilating a boy's genitals is, on the contrary, to turn him into a violence-object, for the meaning of this ordeal for the boy (in most cultures that practice such initiation rites) is to challenge him to develop and demonstrate the physical courage and the ability to tolerate physical pain and injury that are a prerequisite for being a warrior, that is, a violence-object. It is through passing this test, without flinching, crying, or fleeing, that he proves he has become a man (that is, someone who is brave enough to let himself become a violence-object); for that he will be honored, just as he will be shamed (treated as not a "real man") for showing any signs of pain or fear.

Homophobia

Another closely related source of violence is homophobia, by which I mean the attitude of fear, hatred, and contempt for homosexuality and homosexuals. The reason for homophobia has long been recognized as the fear that one is, or is thought to be, homosexual oneself, which to the homophobic person is a source of intolerable shame, and motivates behavior designed to prove one's heterosexuality. This is particularly likely to result in violence when the homophobic person is a man, because the most direct defense against the fear that one is or could be suspected of being homosexual is to engage in an exaggeration of the heterosexual sex-role stereotype; and since violence is part of that definition of masculinity, exaggerated masculinity is likely to take the form of exaggerated violence.

Defenses against the fear of being or appearing to be homosexual may take a variety of other forms besides violence, of course, such as sexual promiscuity (in men, the "Don Juan" syndrome—although it should be remembered that the original Don Juan committed both rape and murder), "machismo" (of which violence is only one component), and the avoidance of anything that resembles the feminine sex-role stereotype, such as tenderness, intimacy, nurturance, passivity, dependency, forgiveness, and the capacity to feel anything, physical or emotional, including pain, fear, depression, love, compassion, vulnerability, sadness.

The only feeling that many violent men will let themselves feel is anger (rage, hate). That this is the emotion that most closely and directly precedes and stimulates violent behavior is hardly surprising, of course. What I was surprised to observe, however, in the most "macho" and violent men I worked with, was that they would not allow themselves to have even that feeling. Perhaps this was because being angry reveals that you have something to be angry about, and is too revealing of the fact that you can be hurt by others. Thus, the motto of the most violent men of all could be summarized in the aphorism, "Don't get mad, get even." Violence is most common when both the shame and the rage that causes it are unacknowledged (even to the self, so that both feelings are effectively unconscious).

The psychodynamic logic that makes homophobia a generator of violence rests on the fact that the most direct and concrete ways to prove that one does not love men are to murder men and rape women. These communicate the messages: "I do not love men, I hate them, and to prove that I will show you how much I hate them, by killing them," and, "I do not desire men sexually, I desire women, and to prove that I will show you how much I desire them, by raping them."

I emphasize the importance and centrality of homophobia as a cause of male violence because I was confronted with evidence of it on a daily basis in my work with the most violent men our society produces, in the most violent environment, the prison. This is an environment that stimulates homophobia, given the high incidence of the rape of male prisoners by other male prisoners, most of whom would kill you if you made the mistake of imagining that their raping other men meant that they themselves were "gay". For example, there are few psychological crises in a male prisoner's life that are more likely to result in his going "berserk" and assaulting everyone in his environment than the phenomenon called "homosexual panic," a mental state that includes the fear that he is surrounded by homosexual men who are bent on raping him or turning him into a homosexual or a woman. Conflicts over homosexuality (both intra-psychic and interpersonal) have been reported by most observers, myself included, to be among the main causes of the homicides that occur in prisons.

But it would be a mistake to think that the homophobia that these men experienced, and to which they responded by becoming violent, was simply a rational response to the real danger of being raped by other men in the unique environment of the prison. For many of the murders that these men had committed in the community, before they had ever been inside a prison, revolved around the same issue. One man who had run away from home at the age of twelve after his abusive, alcoholic father attacked him with a butcher knife had found no way to support himself on the streets except by working as a male prostitute. After some years of that, a man that he picked up made the mistake of assuming that the fact that he worked as a male prostitute meant that he was gay. His response was immediate and lethal: killing the man was the only way he could imagine to prove that he was heterosexual.

But even in cases where the link to homophobia is not so immediate and obvious, I am convinced that homophobia underlies most male violence. I say that because, as I explained in my earlier book, violence is to behavior what paranoia is to thoughts. Violence is the behavioral equivalent of paranoia, the acting out of the core delusion that other people are dangerous to oneself and that one can only defend oneself by attacking or even killing them. (That is why what looks like offensive violence to observers always feels like self-defense to the violent person.) I believe that Freud was profoundly correct when he traced the etiology of paranoia to homophobia, in which the paranoid delusion is a defense against a shame-provoking perception of oneself as homosexual. The thought-processes that produce paranoid delusions, as Freud saw, consist of denial and projection: denial that "I love him" by reversing it into "I hate him," and projection of that thought onto the other person, reversing "I hate him" into "He hates me."

Homophobia, patriarchal or "sexist" attitudes (with a devaluation of everything "female" and an overvaluation of everything "masculine"), a defensive exaggeration of the male gender role, in the form of a kind of hyper-masculinity or "machismo," and the constant threat or reality of violence: I have never seen such an intensification of all those attitudes as I did in the prisons. In fact, the prisons were not only a pure culture of violence, as I said earlier, but also a pure culture of patriarchy, machismo, and homophobia. Since all these attitudes seemed to group themselves together and to reinforce each other, thus forming a syndrome, and since their defensive purpose seemed so transparent (namely, to reassure the individual that he is a real man, whose sexual adequacy as a man cannot be doubted), I could not help but conclude that perhaps homophobia also underlies the whole value system and cultural pattern that we call patriarchy. This includes the exaggerated polarization of gender roles—the purpose of which is clearly to prove something that would need no proof if it were not doubted, namely, that "men are men and women are women, and never the twain shall meet." Prisons are, among other things, a microcosm of the society that produces them, but a microcosm in which some of the problems that exist in the society at large are so concentrated, distilled, and exaggerated that we can see more clearly there some of the uglier, or at least more dangerous and destructive aspects of our society.

CHAPTER 4

A NEW THEORY OF VIOLENCE

One of the advantages of the theory of violence proposed in this book is that it is capable of explaining two paradoxical facts that would otherwise be difficult to account for. The first is that while there are correlations between lower social class and caste status, youth, and masculine gender on the one hand, and violence on the other, it is clear that most of those who are poor, young, and/or male, never commit a serious act of violence in their entire lives.

This paradoxical finding raises the question: are relative poverty, discrimination on the basis of age and race, and sexual asymmetry causes of violence, or do they merely correlate statistically with some other factor that does cause violence? The theory presented here implies that it is not poverty, racism, sexism, or age-discrimination, as such, that actually cause violence. It is, rather, that each correlates with violence because each increases the statistical probability that individuals exposed to these social forces will be subjected to intolerable and potentially self-destroying intensities of shame, from which they do not perceive themselves as having any means of rescuing themselves except by violence—preferably toward others, as in homicide, but also toward themselves, as in suicide, when homicide is not perceived as being possible, or likely to succeed in reducing the shame to tolerable levels.

These pathogenic social forces can be considered risk factors for violence. They increase the risk that the person exposed to them will be subjected to a loading of disrespect that will overwhelm his capacity to find non-violent means of maintaining his self-respect. These considerations are relevant to the search for means of preventing violence, for they suggest that we look not only for ways to reduce the degree to which people are exposed to those risk factors, but also for ways to identify and augment whatever psychological, social or even biological protective factors could neutralize the risk factors.

The second fact that this theory can explain is that some people who are not poor, young, male, or members of minority groups do commit serious violence. Clearly, therefore, some other factor must also be capable of causing violence. Thus, not only are poverty, racism and the other risk factors not sufficient to cause violence, they are also not necessary. The theory presented here can be summarized in the proposition that the cause of violence is not, for example, poverty as such, but rather, that there is a correlation between poverty and violence, because both are correlated, statistically (but only statistically) with the real cause of violence, which is overwhelming and otherwise inescapable and ineradicable shame. Two corollaries follow:

1 Any of the other means (in addition to class, caste and age stratification and sexual asymmetry) by which people can be exposed to overwhelming and inescapable shame (and there are many) can also cause violence.

2 Any factor that reduces the shame-inducing effect of, say, relative poverty, unemployment, lower caste status, youth or male gender, can protect the person from being overwhelmed by shame, and can hence reduce the probability that he will resort to violence.

Violence, like all behavior and all disease, is multi-determined, i.e. it is the product of the interaction between a multiplicity of biological, psychological and social causes, or variables (for example, male sex hormones, child abuse, and relative poverty) each of which can be shown to have the effect of increasing or decreasing the frequency and severity of violence, when all the other variables are held constant. However, beneath all that there are certain regularities and unities, one of which is that shame is a necessary (but not a sufficient) cause of violence, in the same sense that the tubercle bacillus is a necessary (but not a sufficient) cause of tuberculosis. Feelings of shame (versus their opposite, pride) tend to revolve around the question of perceived sexual adequacy (or inadequacy), so that almost any experience that can leave a man feeling ashamed does so by leaving him feeling that he is something less than a man. My point is that in the type of culture called patriarchy, "man" means adult (rather than a boy), potent (rather than impotent), courageous (rather than a wimp or a coward), active (rather than passive), heterosexual (rather than homosexual), masculine (rather than feminine), "ballsy" (rather than castrated or a eunuch), a master rather than a slave, financially successful rather than poor, etc. For example, for many a man the most painful aspect of being poor is that it means he is not an adequate man, not a "real" man—and that image of the man who is not really a man easily melds into the image of the gay man.

When I suggest that homophobia is so central that it is, like shame, virtually universally present wherever violence occurs, I am trying to suggest that for men under patriarchy, the image or concept of "homosexuality" functions as a kind of universal symbol or equivalent of every form of masculine sexual inadequacy; that it therefore epitomizes every cause of shame; and that there are few self-images that cause patriarchally conditioned men to feel shame more deeply than the perception (by themselves or others) that they might be "gay." Many men will resort to almost any degree of violence if that is what it takes for them to ward off that perception of themselves. But the underlying issue is still shame—shame over being an inadequate man, or a non-man, someone who is not "really" a man.

The American High School Massacres

There is a paradox at the heart of the series of mass murders that occurred in high schools throughout the United States during the last years of the twentieth century. These massacres puzzled many people, and were difficult for many theories of violence to explain, because the perpetrators were middle class or even very affluent white youths; they were neither poor nor black. It is true that they possessed two risk factors, namely, being young and male, which is statistically true of most violence; but they violated the statistical generalization that direct interpersonal violence toward others is most common among those who are of lower class and caste status. So why did they commit such horrific violence? The answer is clear, given the points made earlier—they felt overwhelmingly humiliated by being cast in an inferior role. In every single case, the high school mass murderers are described, or described themselves, as feeling shamed by being rejected, ostracized, taunted, teased, mocked, ridiculed, bullied, insulted, disrespected, and/or publicly accused of possessing traits that they found shameful (such as homosexuality). For the sake of brevity, I will mention details from only two of these mass murders. I was personally involved in one of them after the lawyer of one of the perpetrators contacted me because his client "walked right out of" my book *Violence*. The other is the Littleton, Colorado tragedy—quotations from the diaries, video-tapes and websites of the perpetrators were later published. But I would emphasize that the same principles apply to all of them, to the extent that details of each have been made publicly available.

Two other facts about these mass murders are also worth noticing. The first is that they were highly unusual: for the vast majority of American teenagers, the safest places in the community are their schools, where lethal violence is much rarer than on the city streets or even in their homes. The second is that the main reason these highly unusual and atypical events received so much attention in the mass media is because they were so atypical in another respect: they involved white middle-class youngsters. Black teenagers have been killing each other at incomparably higher rates for decades (seven to ten times as often), but the media have for the most part devoted little or no soul-searching to this violence; rather, it has tended to be taken for granted as just what "those people" do, or treated as if it were as unavoidable a characteristic of their nature as, say, monsoons are of the South China Sea. But let a white middle-class child kill his classmates and suddenly we perceive the Decline of the West all over again! These distortions in popular perceptions of violence in America are important not only in themselves, however, but also because the very fact that these distortions exist and are so widespread in our culture and in our media can help us to understand the atypical violence of the white middle-class students themselves, as I will attempt to show.

To protect the confidentiality of the forensic psychiatric interviews with the first of the high-school shooters, I will call him Tommy (not his real name), and I will intermingle quotations from the reports submitted by five clinicians who interviewed him. Tommy was a teenage American high school student who killed and wounded several of his classmates in the late 1990s, following which he cried out, "Kill me now!" When he was interviewed by a detective, he was at first unable to explain why he had done this, and then blurted out, "I guess I just got mad 'cause everybody kept making fun of me." Later interviews with psychiatrists and psychologists revealed the extent both of his anger and of the teasing that contributed to it: Tommy's "early memories of school centered on themes of being taunted"; "kids continued to pick on him when he began high school"; "extensive harassment in which he was called gay, faggot, nerd, geek, and pussy. He stated that he was also spat upon"; "the harassment became particularly pernicious" following publication of a false rumor in the school newspaper that he was having a homosexual relationship with another student.

He was humiliated by the allegation, particularly when other students began to tease him and call him "gay" and "faggot" almost daily. . . . He said that kids would call him gay because he didn't like to be mean to girls. . . . He felt that his peers began to assault his masculinity because in his view he wasn't "mean enough." . . .He's not had any sexual experiences and said that kids make fun of him because of this. . . .His anger over rejections and humiliation mounted. He then hit upon the solution that an act of violence would change the way kids perceived him in school and give him the recognition and acceptance he longed for. . . . He found the. . .idea of shooting students and taking over the school compelling. He imagined that he would gain the respect and awe, if not admiration, of other students. No one would tease him or humiliate him again. . . . He said what he really wanted was more respect from the kids. . . . He repeatedly said that at the time of the shooting the thought which kept running through his mind was, "You've got to do this for yourself." . . .There is probably no better indication of the subjective distress [Tommy] experienced before the shooting than the statement he made that prison would be better than what he was going through, because at least the teasing would stop. . . . He thought that if he got into trouble he would not lose that much because "I didn't have that much. I didn't feel as if anyone really liked me." . . .He reported that he was "tired of people making fun of me, [I] couldn't stand it any more. If I shot one of them or scared them all, they would leave me alone."

When he actually brought his guns to school, a friend of his was so impressed he said "You got the biggest balls here." He felt he could not change his mind, because "the boys would laugh at him for bringing the guns if he did not go ahead with the plans" to use them. Ironically, his plan for gaining respect through violence turned out to be more successful than any other strategy had up to that point, for he said that after the incident, "People respect me now." He reported that "he liked the juvenile detention home better than high school, that the kids were nicer to him, he was not being teased or put down." The tragedy, of course, is that neither he nor the adults responsible for him found any less destructive way to enable him to diminish or tolerate the over-whelming shame and humiliation he had been experiencing.

The story of the massacre at Columbine High School in Littleton, Colorado is virtually identical to that of the one Tommy committed. The two killers, Eric Harris and Dylan Klebold, were subjected to repeated taunting, teasing, insults, name-calling, rejection, and accusations (apparently false) of being homosexual. A journalist with the *New York Times* (25 April 1999) reported:

> The preps and jocks who rule the school taunted the group in the hallways with sarcastic jibes. . . . One member [of the "Trenchcoat Mafia"] was quoted in today's *Denver Post* as saying that they had been pushed against lockers and had rocks and lunchroom mashed potatoes thrown in their faces by jocks.
> (Jodi Wilgoran, "Clique's Dark Journey Began With Black Coat.")

And these allegations were confirmed by many of the "jocks," the athletes at the top of the school's social hierarchy, just as the shooters were at the bottom of it. One football player was quoted as saying:

Columbine is a clean, good place except for those rejects. Most kids didn't want them there. . . . Sure, we teased them. But what do you expect with kids who come to school with weird hairdos and horns on their hats? It's not just jocks; the whole school's disgusted with them. They're a bunch of homos grabbing each other's private parts. If you want to get rid of someone, usually you tease 'em. So the whole school would call them homos.

(Nancy Gibbs and Timothy Roche, "The Columbine Tapes," *Time,* 20 December 1999)

The effect of this on Harris and Klebold, judging from what they wrote, said and did, was shame, leading to rage, leading to violence, in a desperate attempt to replace shame with respect so as to stop the social and psychological annihilation they were undergoing. The tragedy was that neither of them found a way to rescue his self-esteem, and hence his self, except at the expense of his body (his physical survival), and the bodies and physical survival of others. They made it very clear in their websites, videotapes and diaries what their feelings, motives and intentions were. In one videotape, for example, Eric Harris said, "Isn't it fun to get the respect that we're going to deserve?", while holding the sawed-off shotgun he would use at Columbine. And in his website he wrote, "God I can't wait till I can kill you people. I'll just go to some downtown area and blow up and shoot everything I can. Feel no remorse, no sense of shame. I don't care if I live or die in the shootout, all I want to do is kill and injure as many of you as possible." (*New York Times,* 1 May 1999.) It is noteworthy that he combines four themes in these remarks:

1 The need to gain respect.

2 The absence of feelings of remorse, or guilt. Violence always represents self-defense to those who engage in it—defense of that vulnerable and threatened psychological construct, the self. Furthermore, any experience that specifically intensifies feelings of shame simultaneously diminishes feelings of guilt and remorse.

3 Absence of feelings of shame over the plan to kill everyone. Violence, from the point of view of those who engage in it, does not intensify shame, it diminishes it and even reverses it into its opposite, namely, self-respect, and respect from others, which is why the most violent people boast of their violence rather than apologizing for it.

4 The willingness to sacrifice one's body when that is seen as the only means by which one can rescue one's soul (or psyche, or self). Or, when one's self has already died, to kill one's body as well (along with other people's), since that may be seen as the only means of escape from an intolerable degree of shame.

One lesson the Columbine tragedy teaches is that lower social class and caste status are far from being the only determinants of over-whelming shame (though they are the most common epidemi-ologically). At Columbine, where everyone was of the same social class and caste, the criteria for social status involved not money or "race," but athletic ability and the kinds of social skills needed for popularity in that particular school, in both of which Harris and Klebold were sadly and even tragically deficient.

But there is an irony in this tragedy which is too important to over-look. The irony is that the main reason why communities like Littleton and schools like Columbine exist is to enable the families who move to those school districts to benefit from their high social and economic status and enjoy freedom from poverty and degradation, and from the violence that poverty and degradation bring with them, while leaving the class and caste structure of our society as a whole intact. They are rescuing themselves at the expense of those who are poor and/or colored, and in effect abandoning them to those war-zones of almost unlimited violence, the inner-city ghettos into which the "underclass" is segregated in the American version of apartheid. As one of the Columbine football players said after the massacre, "I thought we lived in a bubble." (Sara Rimer, "The School: Good Grades, Good Teams and Some Bad Feelings," New York Times, 22 April 1999.) And they were living in a bubble—an enclave of privilege, affluence, and advantage from which the poor and weak were excluded. The problem was, however, that violence, which they had tried to eliminate by living only among others of the same class and caste status, followed them right into that bubble. And of course it was inevitable, for even by calling Littleton a bubble, the student who used that word indicated that he knew that something very different existed outside it, namely, a world that was not so privileged. So Littleton, which superficially resembled a "classless" society, was in fact the product of the most extreme development of the system of class stratification, namely, the rigid segregation of breathtakingly affluent suburbs from wretchedly poor, virtually uninhabitable inner-city ghettos.

I do not say this with any sense of self-righteousness, for like most upper-middle-class professionals I have done exactly the same thing myself, in the effort to provide my children and myself with the best possible education and the highest possible degree of freedom from crime and violence. I am merely insisting that we cannot even begin to prevent violence until we can acknowledge what we ourselves are doing that contributes to it, actively or passively, and to remember that in a democracy we are all responsible for all. What that means is that if we want to prevent or at least diminish the violence to which we are all vulnerable, even in affluent communities like Littleton, then it is essential that we do not cease to work toward true social and economic equality throughout our society. Otherwise the violence that we moved to our version of Littleton to escape, will follow us right into the bubble that we had thought would be safe. For what Littleton did was to reproduce the very status hierarchy that it was meant as an escape from, albeit one that was governed by different criteria.

Why did it do that? Or to be more exact, how could it have avoided doing that? It is a question of values. To the extent that we place a positive value on social stratification and hierarchies, whether actively or passively, then we signal to our children that status systems are a good thing, and they are likely then to reproduce their own versions.

Working to dismantle all status hierarchies, however, does not at all require that we stop making distinctions between better or worse quality work, whether in the arts, the sciences, or any other field of endeavor. We have to recognize that the only basis on which we can live with each other without violence is one of mutual respect, a respect that is so deep and unconditional that it is not dependent on achievement or behavior, but is respect for human dignity, for the inviolability of the human soul and personality, and a determination not to subject anyone to any shame that is not an unavoidable consequence of the fact that we are all imperfect and therefore will all inevitably and appropriately suffer the narcissistic wound of acknowledging our own imperfections. Finally, it is important to remember Malcolm X's insight that no one can give someone else self-esteem or self-respect; people can only acquire that for themselves, through their own achievements and way of life. But we can choose whether we make available the tools people need to acquire their own self-esteem, by deciding whether to do everything possible to guarantee true equality of opportunity, including equal access to education.

Thus it is not enough to provide schools like Columbine High only for the children of the affluent white upper-middle class. It is just as essential to provide schools of equal quality for every child everywhere, for failure to do so sends a message to all our children, both those in the ghetto and those in the Columbines of the world. This message is that creating status hierarchies that expose those at the bottom to soul-destroying, violence-provoking intensities of humiliation is acceptable human behavior.

Unemployment

This theory of violence can also explain why there is no one-to-one relationship between unemployment and violence, even though there is in general a statistical correlation between the two. For example, if unemployment is among the "causes" of violence, why was the murder rate ten times higher in the United States than in the United Kingdom and the rest of Western Europe during the 1980s and most of the 1990s, when the unemployment rate was two or three times as high in the U.K. and Europe as it was in the U.S? The answer, of course, is that it is not unemployment as such that causes violence; what causes violence, rather, is the loss of self-esteem and feelings of self-worth, the blow especially to one's sense of adequacy as a man (men are, after all, expected to be the "breadwinners" and to "bring home the bacon" in all patriarchal cultures), and the shame brought on by rejection and enforced passivity and dependency, which can all be precipitated by being fired from one's job. Can be, but are not necessarily. For the psychological meaning of unemployment is shaped both by the psychological strengths and vulnerabilities of the individual, and by the meanings that it is given by the culture in which the individual lives—as embodied and symbolized, for example, by the way in which the society responds economically and in terms of moral value judgments to those who are unemployed.

Katherine S. Newman, a Harvard anthropologist, has written a brilliant exposition of the degree—unique among the developed nations of the world—to which American culture shames and stigmatizes the unemployed (*No Shame In My Game: The Working Poor in the Inner City,* 1999). As she puts it:

Americans have always been committed to the moral maxim that work defines the person. . . . Given our tradition of equating moral value with employment, it stands to reason that the most profound dividing line in our culture is that separating the working person from the unemployed. . . .We attribute a whole host of moral virtues to those who have found and kept a job, almost any job, and dismiss those who haven't as slothful or irresponsible.We inhabit an unforgiving culture that is blind to the many reasons why some people cross that employment barrier and others are left behind. We express this view in a variety of ways in our social policies. Virtually all our benefits (especially health care but including unemployment insurance, life insurance, child care tax credits, etc.) are provided through the employment system. In Western Europe this is often not the case: health care is provided directly through the tax system and benefits come to people who are political "citizens" whether they work or not. In the U.S., however, those outside the employment system are categorized as unworthy and made to feel it by excluding them from these systems of support. To varying degrees, we "take care" of the socially excluded by creating stigmatized categories for their benefits— welfare and Medicaid [an inferior grade of health insurance] being prime

examples. Yet we never confuse the approved, acceptable Americans with
the undeserving, and we underscore the difference by separating them
into different bureaucratic worlds.... From the earliest beginnings of
the nation, work has been the *sine qua non* of membership in this society.
We are so divided in other domains—race, geography, and the like—that
common ground along almost any other lines is difficult to achieve....
The French, by contrast, are French whether they work or not.

In other words, people who happen to be unemployed are shamed
more severely in the U.S. than in western Europe in two ways: not only
are they given relatively lower levels of financial support for shorter
periods of time, but the very way in which that support is legally and
bureaucratically structured and defined is more stigmatizing. This is
not to say that it is not humiliating to be fired or laid off from one's job,
or unable to find employment, in any society. Nor am I suggesting that
the tendency within a nation for rates of criminal and political violence
to increase or decrease over time as the unemployment rate rises or
falls is exclusive to the United States; it is not. I am merely suggesting
that it is not surprising that the United States suffers vastly higher
rates of violence than are seen in western Europe even when it is suffering lower levels of unemployment than they are; for there are many
other social, economic and cultural variables besides unemployment
that influence the degree to which the members of any given society
are exposed to shame.

Single-Parent Families

Another factor that correlates with rates of violence in the United
States is the rate of single-parent families: children raised in them are
more likely to be abused, and are more likely to become delinquent
and criminal as they grow older, than are children who are raised by
two parents. For example, over the past three decades those two variables—the rates of violent crime and of one-parent families—have
increased in tandem with each other; the correlation is very close. For
some theorists, this has suggested that the enormous increase in the
rate of youth violence in the U.S. over the past few decades has been

caused by the proportionately similar increase in the rate of single-parent families.

As a parent myself, I would be the first to agree that child-rearing is such a complex and demanding task that parents need all the help they can get, and certainly having two caring and responsible parents available has many advantages over having only one. In addition, children, especially boys, can be shown to benefit in many ways, including diminished risk of delinquency and violent criminality, from having a positive male role-model in the household. The adult who is most often missing in single-parent families is the father. Some criminologists have noticed that Japan, for example, has practically no single-parent families, and its murder rate is only about one-tenth as high as that of the United States.

Sweden's rate of one-parent families, however, has grown almost to equal that in the United States, and over the same period (the past few decades), yet Sweden's homicide rate has also been on average only about one-tenth as high as that of the U.S., during that same time. To understand these differences, we should consider another variable, namely, the size of the gap between the rich and the poor. As stated earlier, Sweden and Japan both have among the lowest degrees of economic inequity in the world, whereas the U.S. has the highest polarization of both wealth and income of any industrialized nation. And these differences exist even when comparing different family structures. For example, as Timothy M. Smeeding has shown, the rate of relative poverty is very much lower among single-parent families in Sweden than it is among those in the U.S. Even more astonishing, however, is the fact that the rate of relative poverty among single-parent families in Sweden is much lower than it is among two-parent families in the United States ("Financial Poverty in Developed Countries," 1997). Thus, it would seem that however much family structure may influence the rate of violence in a society, the overall social and economic structure of the society—the degree to which it is or is not stratified into highly polarized upper and lower social classes and castes—is a much more powerful determinant of the level of violence.

There are other differences between the cultures of Sweden and the U.S. that may also contribute to the differences in the correlation between single-parenthood and violent crime. The United States, with its strongly Puritanical and Calvinist cultural heritage, is much more intolerant of both economic dependency and out-of-wedlock sex than Sweden. Thus, the main form of welfare support for single-parent families in the U.S. (until it was ended a year ago) A.F.D.C., Aid to Families with Dependent Children, was specifically denied to families in which the father (or any other man) was living with the mother; indeed, government agents have been known to raid the homes of single mothers with no warning in the middle of the night in order to "catch" them in bed with a man, so that they could then deprive them (and their children) of their welfare benefits. This practice, promulgated by politicians who claimed that they were supporting what they called "family values," of course had the effect of destroying whatever family life did exist. Fortunately for single mothers in Sweden, the whole society is much more tolerant of people's right to organize their sexual life as they wish, and as a result many more single mothers are in fact able to raise their children with the help of a man.

Another difference between Sweden and the U.S. is that fewer single mothers in Sweden are actually dependent on welfare than is true in the U.S. The main reason for this is that mothers in Sweden receive much more help from the government in getting an education, including vocational training; more help in finding a job; and access to high-quality free childcare, so that mothers can work without leaving their children uncared for. The U.S. system, which claims to be based on opposition to dependency, thus fosters more welfare dependency among single mothers than Sweden's does, largely because it is so more miserly and punitive with the "welfare" it does provide. Even more tragically, however, it also fosters much more violence. It is not single motherhood as such that causes the extremely high levels of violence in the United States, then; it is the intense degree of shaming to which single mothers and their children are exposed by the punitive, miserly, Puritanical elements that still constitute a powerful strain in the culture of the United States.

CHAPTER 5

HOW TO CREATE LESS VIOLENT SOCIETIES

The first step toward learning how to prevent any health problem is to discover what causes it, so that we know what causes need to be removed or neutralized. That is why I discussed the causes of violence at such length in the previous chapters. Once we know the causes, we can apply that knowledge to the issue of prevention in a very direct way: we can stop causing it. We know how to cause violence: by shaming people. Therefore we know how to prevent it: stop shaming them. That does not mean that we either can or should eliminate shame from the world, for the capacity to experience feelings of shame is as necessary as the capacity to experience physical pain. Just as physical pain signals to us that there is a threat to our physical health, so shame warns us that there is something lacking in our repertoire of social or cognitive skills and knowledge, some failure of development and maturation that needs further work. But unless we provide people with access to the means by which they can develop and mature further, such as education and employment, we leave them with no means other than violence, of protecting themselves from potentially overwhelming and intolerable feelings of shame .

We know how people shame other people, namely, by treating them as inferior, on an individual scale, or by assigning them to an inferior social and economic status on a collective scale. Not everyone who is shamed in these ways will become violent, because most people have enough independent sources of self-esteem and self-respect to withstand even fairly intense disrespect from others. But if the goal is to start a fight, that is the one method that is most guaranteed to work with whoever is vulnerable to becoming violent. Thus, the first steps toward preventing violence consist of not shaming people (as by disrespecting them), and not depriving them of access to the tools they need in order to attain and maintain their self-respect even when they are disrespected by others.

The most important implication this has for the issue of preventing violence is that violence does not occur spontaneously, it occurs only when we cause it; so that the task of preventing violence does not so much require us to do something special, as it requires us to *stop* doing the things we have been doing that cause violence; in other words, to discontinue the individual and social practices and behaviors that have been shown to cause violence. Once we stop causing violence, it will disappear by itself.

That simple statement is not as optimistic as it may sound, however, because it is not at all clear how many of those things people will be willing to stop doing even if they can be convinced that they cause violence. For preventing violence is not the only goal that many people value, and there are many other goals that some value more. As Elliott Currie wrote:

> We have the level of criminal violence we do because we have arranged our social and economic life in certain ways rather than others. The brutality and violence of American life are a signal that there are profound social costs to maintaining those arrangements. But by the same token, altering them also has a price; and if we continue to tolerate the conditions that have made us the most violent of industrial societies, it is not because the problem is overwhelmingly mysterious or because we do not know what to do, but because we have decided that the benefits of changing those conditions aren't worth the costs.
>
> (*Confronting Crime*, 1985)

It is very important to note, however, that the only segment of the population for whom changing our social and economic conditions in the ways that prevent violence would exact a higher cost would be the extremely wealthy upper, or ruling, class—the wealthiest one per cent of the population (which in the United States today controls some 39 per cent of the total wealth of the nation, and 48 per cent of the financial wealth, as shown by Wolff in *Top Heavy* (1996). The other 99 per cent of the population—namely, the middle class and the lower class—would benefit, not only from decreased rates of violence (which primarily victimize the very poor), but also from a more equitable distribution of the collective wealth and income of our unprecedentedly wealthy societies. Even on a worldwide scale, it would require a remarkably small sacrifice from the wealthiest individuals and nations to raise everyone on earth, including the populations of the poorest nations, above the subsistence level, as the United Nations *Human Development Report 1998,* has shown. I emphasize the wealthiest individuals as well as nations because, as the U.N. Report documents, a tiny number of the wealthiest individuals actually possess wealth on a scale that is larger than the annual income of most of the nations of the earth. For example, the *three* richest *individuals* on earth have assets that exceed the combined Gross Domestic Product of the *forty-eight* poorest *countries!* The assets of the 84 richest individuals exceed the Gross Domestic Product of the most populous nation on earth, China, with 1.2 billion inhabitants. The 225 richest individuals have a combined wealth of over $1 trillion, which is equal to the annual income of the poorest 47 per cent of the world's population, or 2.5 billion people. By comparison:

> It is estimated that the additional cost of achieving and maintaining universal access to basic education for all, basic health care for all, reproductive health care for all women, adequate food for all and safe water and sanitation for all is roughly $40 billion a year. This is less than 4 per cent of the combined wealth of the 225 richest people in the world.
>
> *(U.N.H.D.R. 1998)*

It has been shown throughout the world, both internationally and intranationally, that reducing economic inequities not only improves physical health and reduces the rate of death from natural causes far more effectively than doctors, medicines and hospitals; it also decreases the rate of death from both criminal and political violence far more effectively than any system of police forces, prisons, or military interventions ever invented. My goal in writing this book is simply to make sure that all who read it will learn which choices lead to more violence and which ones to less, so that whatever choices they make will at least be made with full knowledge of the costs and benefits.

It may seem obvious that violence can be caused, but what reason do we have to think that it can be prevented? One reason for believing that is because it is already being prevented, or has been prevented, in all those nations, cultures and periods of history that have lower rates of violence than other nations or epochs.

Social and Political Democracy

Since the end of the Second World War, the homicide rates of the nations of western Europe, and Japan, for example, have been only about a tenth as high as those of the United States, which is another way of saying that they have been preventing 90 per cent of the violence that the U.S still experiences. Their rates of homicide were not lower than those in the U.S. before. On the contrary, Europe and Asia were scenes of the largest numbers of homicides ever recorded in the history of the world, both in terms of absolute numbers killed and in the death rates per 100,000 population, in the "thirty years' war" that lasted from 1914 to 1945. Wars, and governments, have always caused far more homicides than all the individual murderers put together (Richardson, *Statistics of Deadly Quarrels*, 1960; Keeley, *War Before Civilization*, 1996.) After that war ended, however, they all took two steps which have been empirically demonstrated throughout the world to prevent violence. They instituted social democracy (or "welfare states," as they are sometimes called), and achieved an unprecedented decrease in the inequities in wealth and income between the richest and poorest groups in the population, one effect of which is to reduce the frequency of interpersonal or "criminal" violence. And Germany, Japan and Italy adopted political democracy as well, the effect of which is to reduce the frequency of international violence, or warfare (including "war crimes").

While the United States adopted political democracy at its inception, it is the only developed nation on earth that has never adopted social democracy (a "welfare state"). The United States alone among the developed nations does not provide universal health insurance for all its citizens; it has the highest rate of relative poverty among both children and adults, and the largest gap between the rich and the poor, of any of the major economies; vastly less adequate levels of unemployment insurance and other components of shared responsibility for human welfare; and so on. Thus, it is not surprising that it also has murder rates that have been five to ten times as high as those of any other developed nation, year after year. It is also consistent with that analysis that the murder rate finally fell below the epidemic range in which it had fluctuated without exception for the previous thirty years (namely, 8 to 11 homicides per 100,000 population per year), only in 1998, after the unemployment rate reached its lowest level in thirty years and the rate of poverty among the demographic groups most vulnerable to violence began to diminish—slightly—for the first time in thirty years.

Some American politicians, such as President Eisenhower, have suggested that the nations of western Europe have merely substituted a high suicide rate for the high homicide rate that the U.S. has. In fact, the suicide rates in most of the other developed nations are *also* substantially lower than those of the United States, or at worst not substantially higher. The suicide rates throughout the British Isles, the Netherlands, and the southern European nations are around one-third *lower* than those of the U.S.; the rates in Canada, Australia, and New Zealand, as well as Norway and Luxembourg, are about the same. Only the remaining northern and central European countries and Japan have suicide rates that are higher, ranging from 30 per cent higher to roughly twice as high as the suicide rate of the U.S. By comparison, the U.S. homicide rate is roughly *ten* times as high as those of western Europe (including the U.K., Scandinavia, France, Germany, Switzerland, Austria), southern Europe, and Japan; and *five* times as high as those of Canada, Australia and New Zealand. No other developed nation has a homicide rate that is even close to that of the U.S.

Another reason for concluding that violence can be prevented, and that we know how to do so, can be found by contrasting the effects of the peace settlement that occurred after the First World War with that which followed the Second. As is well known, the Versailles treaty that the Allied powers imposed on Germany following the end of World War I included not only a statement condemning Germany but also a series of financial penalties so punitive that they would have been ruinous had they been fully enforced. The effect of this was to give the right-wing revanchists (of whom Hitler emerged as the leader) an invaluable propaganda tool, namely, the ability to win elections on the campaign promise to 'undo the shame of Versailles,' i.e. the humiliation to which the Allies had subjected Germany. In fact, even before Hitler entered politics, the great British economist John Maynard Keynes, who was a delegate at the peace conference, saw how destructive the terms of the Versailles settlement would be to the prospects for future peace, so he resigned in protest and wrote an angry denunciation of it, *The Economic Consequences of the Peace*, in which he predicted much of what later happened. It goes without saying that neither Keynes's analysis nor mine has anything to do with condoning or justifying any of Hitler's behavior. The point is simply that if one wants peace, then humiliating and punishing one's former enemy is not the way to reach that goal, for, among other things, it only strengthens the hand of people like Hitler who already want revenge and will gladly use any pretext to get it.

Whether we can attribute the very different outcome that followed the end of the Second World War to the sagacity of those who presided over the terms of the peace, as though they had learned from the mistakes made by those who ended World War I, or whether it was merely a fortunate but coincidental byproduct of the Cold War with the Soviet Union, the lesson we ourselves can learn from the difference between the results of the two peace settlements is not only that violence can be prevented, but that the worst form of violence can be prevented – namely, world war. For after the end of World War II, the Allies, far from humiliating the three Axis powers or punishing them financially by ordering them to pay reparations for their war crimes, actually extended financial support to them to help them rebuild their economies after the devastation of the war, and helped them also to establish stable political democratic institutions for the first time. The result has been more than fifty years of unbroken peace on what had been the bloodiest continent in human history during the previous thirty years.

The Hutterites

Another source of evidence that violence can be prevented comes from the experience of those religious sub-cultures that practice "primitive Christian communism," such as the Anabaptist sects—the Hutterites, Amish, and Mennonites. These are classless societies with essentially no inequities of income or wealth and virtually no private property, since they pool their economic resources and share them equally. They also experience virtually no physical violence, either individual or collective.

The Hutterites, for example, since emigrating from eastern Europe to escape religious persecution around 1874, have lived in communal farms in southern Canada and the north-midwestern United States for more than a century. As strict pacifists, that was their only alternative to extermination. Thus, they have no history of collective violence (warfare). They "consider themselves to live the only true form of Christianity, one which entails communal sharing of property and cooperative production and distribution of goods," as Kaplan and Plaut described them in *Personality in a Communal Society* (1955). That is, they conform to the pattern of the earliest Christian communities, as described in the *Acts of the Apostles* (2: 44–45): "all that believed were together, and had all things common; And sold their possessions and goods, and parted them to all men, as every man had need." As a result, the Hutterites experienced "virtually no differentiation of class, income, or standard of living . . . .This society comes as close to being classless as any we know."(Kaplan and Plaut).

An intensive review by medical and social scientists of their well-documented behavioral history and vital statistics during the century since their arrival in North America reported that "We did not find a single case of murder, assault or rape. Physical aggressiveness of any sort was quite rare." (Eaton and Weil, *Culture and Mental Disorders,*

1955.) Hostetler, writing twenty years later, reported that there still had not been a single homicide in the 100 years since the Hutterites entered North America, and only one suicide in a population of about 21,000 (*Hutterite Society*, 1974).

Kibbutzim

A social and economic experiment that is remarkably similar to the Hutterites (except that its basic ideology is completely secular and atheistic) has been conducted since 1909 in Palestine and, as it later became, Israel, namely, the system of collective settlements, farms and other communally owned economic enterprises called kibbutzim. In these classless societies, of which by the late twentieth century there were roughly 200, with a total population of 100,000, all wealth is held in common, with profits reinvested in the settlement after members have been provided with food, clothing and shelter and with educational and medical services.

The social structure and practices are deliberately designed to maximize the democratic and egalitarian nature of the community. For example, work and occupational roles are structured around the goal of achieving complete equality of the sexes. The education of children is intended to be as permissive and non-authoritarian as possible, in light of Freud's warning as to the harmfulness of authoritarianism toward children. As one observer described kibbutz education, "It does not inculcate a consciousness of sin. . . . It does not regard any instinctive behaviour as intrinsically evil or wicked and rejects corporal punishment as morally wrong and harmful to the child. Kibbutz educators view punishment of any sort as undesirable." The goal is to make the educational system as democratic as possible, so as to achieve "the ideal of educational equality, which is in turn the corollary of social and economic equality." (Muhammad Huq, "History of Education," *Encyclopaedia Britannica*, 1988).

What is striking about most descriptions of kibbutzim is their extreme degree of social and economic equality and classlessness. As Spiro noted in *Kibbutz* (1975), "The kibbutz believes in the principle of 'from each according to his ability, to each according to his need.' "

Another notable feature of the kibbutzim, which has been remarked on by most observers, is the virtually complete absence of violence, crime and delinquency (Bettelheim, *Children of the Dream*, 1969; Fischer and Geiger, *Reform Through Community*, 1991, and *Family, Justice, and Delinquency*, 1995; and Spiro, just cited). A consequence (and perhaps also a cause) of the complete absence of violence is that "in the kibbutz there is no policeman nor anyone like him."

The kibbutzniks are not pacifists, however, and in Arab-Israeli wars have volunteered in disproportionately large numbers for the most dangerous military units. Does that mean that they have merely displaced their violent impulses from each other onto the Arabs? The evidence suggests otherwise. Dar, et al. (*The Imprint of the Intifada*, 2000) report that "research has repeatedly shown that kibbutz youth are distinguished by their tolerance towards Arabs and a pacific approach to the Israeli-Palestinian conflict."

The kibbutzim seem to exemplify two principles (at least): that it is possible to prevent violence, and how to prevent violence.

Immigrants

Another example illustrating both the feasibility and the method of preventing violence is the history of the ethnic groups that have come to the U.S. since the beginning of European colonization, as summarized by Silberman in *Criminal Violence, Criminal Justice* (1978):

> The history of ethnic groups in the United States demonstrates that upward mobility is the most effective cure for criminal violence. In the second half of the nineteenth century, most of the people responsible for street crime were Irish- and German-Americans; in the first half of the twentieth century, they were mostly Italian-, Jewish-, Polish-, and Greek-Americans. The James Q. Wilsons of both periods were certain that reducing poverty would have little effect on crime, since (in their view) the "new immigrants," unlike their predecessors, really preferred their dissolute and crime-ridden way of life. But each of these groups moved out of crime as it moved into the middle class. The same will be true—the same is true—of black Americans; involvement in street crime drops sharply as blacks move into the middle class.

Since Silberman wrote those words, they have been abundantly confirmed, as an unprecedentedly large percentage of African-Americans have entered the middle-class professions: law, medicine, academia, and so on. And while crime and violence continue to plague the black community, it is not the black middle class that is committing it. It is, almost entirely, those who have not (yet) made it into the middle class.

Classless Hunting-and-Gathering Cultures

Further evidence that violence can be prevented comes from cross-cultural anthropological observations, of which I will mention two here. The first is the discovery that there are cultures, although rare, that have little or no violence, with no wars, and few or no homicides. Keeley (*War Before Civilization*, 1996) has been of all anthropologists one of the most skeptical about claims to have discovered a truly peaceful society. Yet even he concludes that there are societies in which there is a virtually complete absence of serious or lethal violence. Among them he includes the Polar Eskimo of northwestern Greenland who "avoided all feuds and armed conflict." He adds that "murder was not unknown" in this society, but was apparently rare. Among other examples of peaceful hunter-gatherers, he mentions that the Mbuti pygmies of central Africa and the Semang of Malaysia "seem to have completely eschewed any form of violent conflict and can legitimately be regarded as pacifistic." He further comments that pacifistic societies also occur (if uncommonly) at every level of social and economic complexity, though he adds that these are less common among societies that have developed agriculture than among the more primitive hunters and gatherers). And he points out that:

> Peaceful societies even exist among industrial states. For example, neither Sweden nor Switzerland has engaged in warfare for nearly two centuries; their homicide rates are among the lowest in the world. Sweden was once home to the legendarily belligerent Vikings and remained one of the most warlike societies in Europe until the 18th century. Nevertheless, Sweden has fought no wars since 1815. Both nations and a few other nations in Asia and South America offer testimony that there is nothing inherently warlike about states. Thus pacifist societies seem to have existed at every

level of social organization, but they are extremely rare and seem to require special circumstances. The examples of Sweden and the Semai [of Malaysia] demonstrate that societies can change from pacifistic to warlike, or vice versa, within a few generations or within the lifetime of an individual. As these cases and the case of the Polar Eskimo establish, the idea that violent conflicts between groups is an inevitable consequence of being human or of social life itself is simply wrong.

Gibson in Haas, *The Anthropology of War* (1990) describes another non-violent society, the Buid, a highland group in Mindoro, the Philippines, who "reject any form of violence, aggression, or even competition." Their economic system is based on equal sharing of wealth, their political system "eliminates competition for power and prestige," and they have "an ideology of ascribed equality: people are considered equal no matter how successful they are in various activities." They disapprove of boastfulness, quarreling, and attempts to dominate others, which they see as leading to violence and murder. To the Buid *maisug*, "aggressive" behavior, connotes everything of negative value in social life, and they regard it as typical of their lowland Christian and Muslim antagonists (both of whom have a historical tradition of exploiting the Buid through trading, raiding and enslaving), whom they hold up as a negative example. Interestingly, the Muslims place a directly opposite value on that same concept. To them, *maisug* "refers to all that is positively valued in men: virility, courage, and the ability to stand up for one's honor." And just as the two groups place opposite values on aggression, so they do on courage, fear, and flight:

> The Buid, by contrast, have no word for "courage," in the sense of
> a positively valued aggressive attitude in the face of physical danger.
> There are many words for fear of and flight from danger, neither
> of which is seen as being reprehensible. Indeed, they are the only
> rational response to danger.

They do not fight wars, and while even their extraordinarily anti-aggressive value system does not render them completely immune from lethal violence, the only known homicide in a ten-year period was committed by an atypical eccentric who had "a fearsome reputation as a sorcerer." Perhaps no social system can guarantee absolute protection from the occasional isolated deviant.

Finally, I will refer back to the cross-cultural statistics summarized in Chapter 2 with reference to the causes of violence. Since there is a reciprocity between causation and prevention, those same statistics show the conditions that prevent violence. These are: economic and political egalitarianism, with classless societies, no slavery or social castes, and minimal hierarchicalization in the political sphere; and relative freedom from the invidious display of wealth, boasting, sensitivity to insult, and other social and cultural characteristics that tend to stimulate shame, envy, and violence.

What is extraordinary about the range of cultures we have discussed so far in this chapter is that for all their variety, ranging from modern (post)-industrial economies to Anabaptist communal farming communities to the most primitive non-literate hunting-and-gathering societies, they have two things in common: in all of them, wealth and political power are shared unusually equitably, and they all have remarkably reduced rates of violence. It would appear that social and political egalitarianism (democracy) serves to diminish both shame and violence quite effectively, across a wide range of differing levels of overall economic and cultural development.

Guaranteed Employment vs. Guaranteed Unemployment

In Chapter 2, we reviewed evidence that unemployment tends to stimulate violence. It is noteworthy that, as the rates of unemployment decline, the rates of violence tend to do so as well. Since violence is multi-determined, the effect of any one variable, such as the unemployment rate, can of course be augmented or diminished by the simultaneous effect of other variables (such as the level of unemployment insurance that is provided). Therefore, the high unemployment rates currently seen in many European countries have still not translated into rates of violence remotely as high as those that are seen in the United States because the social "safety net" protecting workers from falling into poverty is so much more secure in Europe than it is in the United States.

But it is not just the effects of unemployment that can be affected by governmental action; so can the rate of unemployment. For example, for many years in the United States, the Federal Reserve Board has intervened to raise the unemployment rate whenever the "danger" arose that it might get too low! Given the effect this can have on the rates of homicide (and suicide), and the efforts of other branches of the government to lower the homicide rate, it is clear that different branches of the government have been working at cross-purposes. One does not have to assume that the Federal Reserve Board was deliberately trying to keep the murder rate as high as possible—and I do not assume that—in order to note that they could hardly have done anything more effective to that end. Conversely, now that the Federal Reserve Board has finally allowed the unemployment rate to reach a thirty-year low, the murder rate has finally fallen slightly below the epidemic levels of the past thirty years. In fact, it is now almost exactly the same as it was at the last time the unemployment rate was this low.

To the extent that we care about the level of violence in our society, however, it is important to do everything in our power to keep the unemployment rate as low as possible—ideally, to provide full employment for everyone able to work (as Roosevelt attempted during the Depression)—and at least not actually cause unemployment. If there is an unavoidable minimum of unemployment, we must try to mitigate the humiliating effects of not being able to find a job, such as providing enough unemployment insurance to prevent poverty.

Gender Roles and Homophobia

The discussion of gender roles and homophobia in Chapters 2 and 3 has implications for the prevention of violence that I want to emphasize here because I think it has not usually been noticed or acknowledged that decisions we make on these issues can have an impact on the level of violence in our society. The general principle here is clear: anything that will reduce the artificial and exaggerated polarization of gender roles, and the irrational fear, hatred, and contempt felt and expressed toward homosexuals will help to prevent violence, because those are among the main causes of violence—and not only, or even primarily, toward women or gays. In line with my contention that we simply need to stop doing the things we are doing that cause violence, it is relevant to notice that there are now several areas in our public life in which major institutions are actively supporting gender asymmetry and discrimination against homosexuals.

The military still has arbitrary rules that vary people's access to military roles based on their gender or their sexual orientation, rather than on the basis of their individual abilities and wishes. These rules are made by governments (which, in a democracy, means all of us, collectively) and can be repealed by governments. Traditionally, only men were conscripted against their will into the military, and, even after women were allowed to join the military voluntarily, participation in combat was restricted more or less exclusively to men. Both these practices help to maintain the traditional gender-role asymmetries that stimulate and perpetuate violence in society.

Some religious sects restrict access to membership in the clergy, and in some cases to membership in the congregation, based on gender or sexual orientation. While it is not appropriate for the government to repeal these rules, the religious bodies themselves can. Nothing could give more support to the Commandment, "Thou shalt not kill." In debates over these issues it is seldom noticed that they are relevant to the issue of preventing violence.

In my discussion of these issues, I am attempting to focus on actions that could be taken (or rather, violence-provoking policies that could be discontinued) by people in positions of power, in the government, the military, the churches and synagogues and mosques, and so on. I am trying to find the strategic levers in society that influence people's attitudes on a mass scale. The major public institutions of our society serve, as Justice Brandeis said of the government, as the moral teachers of the public: the values that they express through their rules and behaviors cannot help but influence the private behavior of the millions of people who respect those institutions and look to them for guidance as to how to live with other people.

Violence Toward Children

Among the other policies that would prevent violence, and which it is in the power of governments to adopt, eliminating legally permitted or even mandated violence toward children would be high on my list. It is time for every country on earth to follow Sweden and the other northern European countries in declaring it illegal for an adult to strike a child. Children sometimes need to be physically restrained—for example, if they are running into traffic, or are assaulting another child, and will not respond to words alone. But one never needs to strike a child in order to restrain him, or for any other reason. We know that the more children are hit, the more they hit others, and we know that the more they are disciplined with 'love-oriented' techniques and verbal reasoning the less violently they themselves behave, both as children and as adults. Naturally, it goes without saying that even more extreme forms of physical violence toward children, such as genital mutilation and capital punishment, should not be practiced or permitted. The U.K., like every other Western democracy except the U.S., has abolished capital punishment for all ages. Many other countries prescribe the death penalty for adults, but the U.S. is one of only six nations on earth today that still executes children (as young as sixteen). Clearly, discontinuing this policy would end one practice that is a statement to every parent and child in the country that it is morally and legally permissible to express disapproval of children by killing them.

Restricting Media Violence

Messages validating violence are also sent to children and adults through the mass media and video games. There is a firm consensus, on the part of the dozens of behavioral scientists and scientific groups who have investigated the effects on children of violence in the media, that it does stimulate violent behavior in those who are, like many children, not merely exposed to it but saturated with it. Major reviews of studies of this subject have been conducted by virtually every major scientific and professional organization and by the Surgeon General's office, and have reached the same conclusion (Bok, *Mayhem*, 1998).

The public policy dilemma is more difficult: how far to go down the road of government censorship. There are other alternatives. One is to encourage parents to protect their children from this influence with the help of "V-chips" programmed to block reception of violent television programs—though that would be least effective with the most vulnerable children, those with the least caring and resourceful parents. Another is to provide "media literacy" classes in schools, to help children learn how to gain some critical distance from the mindless violence to which they are exposed (not to mention the mindless advertisements). A third is for people to boycott the networks and advertisers who bring this material into people's living rooms, to lobby the network executives, and so on.

In Norway, government censors actively monitor programs and films, and block access to those they deem objectionable. Perhaps that works in Norway, and perhaps it would work in the United Kingdom. But based on how I have seen censorship work in the United States and Canada, when it has been tried, I can only worry that government censors might ban the programs and films that were harmless or even worthwhile, and permit the truly violence-provoking material to be shown. For example, after a Canadian law was passed a few years ago forbidding the sale of pornographic books and magazines, the first thing the censors confiscated were newsletters from a lesbian organization that were purely informational and had no sexual content.

It is also important to remember that it is not violence in the media as such that stimulates violent behavior, but rather, the depiction of violence as entertainment rather than as tragedy. There is as much violence in *Hamlet* or *The Bacchae* as there is in any "spaghetti Western," but it is not watching Shakespeare or Euripides that makes children more violent. The difference, apart from the quality of the writing, is that in serious drama there is never any doubt about the gravity of what is happening and the depth of suffering it causes, which is why those plays elicit empathy and compassion rather than the trivialization of violence into a spectator sport. But could government censors be trusted to recognize the difference?

On the other hand, common sense would suggest that some reasonable compromises should be possible here, and that this is an important enough problem to call for a serious discussion of the widest possible range of solutions. One paradox in current censorship is that we are much more active about restricting access to sexual content than to depictions of violence. Apparently there is a consensus that it is acceptable to allow children to see people murdering or assaulting each other in the most brutal fashion, on a daily basis, whereas it would be morally shocking and unacceptable to allow them to see two people making love. I am not arguing that either kind of program or film is appropriate for a child, but the distinction we are making here seems to say that murder as entertainment is acceptable but sex is not. And since we seem to be able to provide some degree of censorship for the films and programs with overt sexual content, I cannot see why violent content cannot also be restricted to hours or television channels less accessible to children, and why violent films could not be restricted to the age groups that might be less vulnerable or suggestible. Why should we allow children to watch violence when we do not allow them to watch erotica? This is especially paradoxical, since most studies of the effects of non-violent erotica have concluded that exposure to it actually decreases people's predisposition to engage in violent behavior.

The ultimate solution to this problem, though it is a long-term one, would be to increase the level and quality of education for the entire population. The definitive end to the production and distribution of this pornography of violence will occur only when people stop wanting to watch it, and that only when they are well educated enough, and emotionally secure and mature enough, to recognize the difference between mindless mayhem and thoughtful and moving drama.

Gun Control

Great Britain passed a stringent handgun control law not long ago, following the tragic mass shooting at Dunblane in 1996—a very sensible and realistic component, though only one among many, in a national strategy to prevent future violence. If only the United States, which seems to have a new Dunblane of its own every few weeks, could become equally rational. Unfortunately, as most of the rest of the world knows, the United States is in the grip of a national psychosis on the subject of guns – not everyone, but the effective ruling majority. It is a subject on which it is difficult to engage many otherwise reasonable people in a rational discussion. Yet the facts are clear, and there are many that are relevant to this discussion. Incomparably more family members are killed by one of their own family's guns—by accident, suicide, or an impulsive family quarrel—than are killed or even threatened by a criminal's gun. Many people carry guns in order to "protect" themselves; but what the statistics show is that people are much more likely to be killed if they are carrying a gun than if they are not. Between 1984 and 1994 the homicide rate among 14–17-year-olds tripled, and the increase was entirely due to one weapon and one weapon alone—the handgun. The argument that gun ownership by private citizens is either necessary or sufficient to prevent the Federal government from turning into a dictatorship parts company with reality—assault rifles against ballistic missiles, Sherman tanks or hydrogen bombs? Of course people could, and some would, use other weapons if they did not have guns, but that does not undo the fact that fatalities are seven times more likely when the weapon is a gun than when it is a knife.

One of the main obstacles to meaningful gun controls has been the Second Amendment to the U.S. Constitution, which reads in splendid ambiguity. A well regulated militia, being necessary to the security of a free State, the right of the people to keep and bear arms, shall not be infringed. Yet it is not clear why the Second Amendment to the Constitution, ambiguous though it is, continues to be interpreted as forbidding the banning of handguns and assault rifles when it does not stop the government from keeping tanks and machine guns out of private hands. But as long as it continues to be so interpreted, there may be no cure for this national psychosis except to pass a new amendment invalidating it and replacing it with one that will ban guns from private hands. Doing that will not in and of itself stop all violence; if no one had killed anyone with a gun during any recent year, the U.S.

would still have had a higher murder rate than any other developed nation because of all the murders that are already being committed by other weapons. Nevertheless, the vast majority of both homicides and suicides in the U.S. are committed by guns, and removing them from circulation would undoubtedly prevent many impulsive shootings, which are much more likely to terminate in death than are impulsive stabbings or beatings. The main problem, however, is that currently an estimated 200 million or more guns are in circulation in the U.S., and it is not clear how it will be possible to confiscate them all, or even just the handguns and assault rifles before the end of the century. On the other hand, it is worth remembering that Boston was remarkably successful in removing handguns from its inner-city youth by concentrating resources on them as well as on the small handful of gun dealers who were supplying most of the guns to criminals. So it is important not to give up.

Nevertheless, it is more important to change people's motives, their wish to harm someone, and to change the culture of violence and death in the U.S. That is precisely what the process of passing a new Constitutional amendment could accomplish—the cohesion of a new set of cultural values that in turn would help to shape people's motives. The values that support the Second Amendment as it is now interpreted are the same values that support violence in all its forms, Repealing it could be the first step toward forging a new set of values that would embody the Biblical command, "Therefore choose life."

Universal Access to Free Higher Education

Education is one of the most powerful tools for acquiring self-esteem, and since self-esteem is the most powerful psychological force that prevents violence, it is not surprising that level of education is one of the strongest predictors of whether or not a person will be violent.

A few years ago, my colleagues and I conducted a study to determine what programs in the Massachusetts prison system were most effective in preventing recidivism, or reoffending, among prisoners after they are discharged and return to the community. The only one that we found to have been 100 per cent successful, up to that time, was a program of free higher education that enabled prisoners to acquire a college degree. Over a twenty-five-year period, more than 200 inmates, most of whom were serving time for the most serious violent crimes, including murder, rape, and armed robbery, had received a college degree and then left prison, and not one had been returned for a new crime. At first I thought we had made a mistake, and missed someone. Then I discovered that the state of Indiana had found exactly the same result, and so had Folsom State Prison in California—not one prisoner who had acquired a college degree while in prison had been reincarcerated for a new crime.

Now, nothing is 100 per cent forever or under all circumstances, and the success rate for such programs is not that high everywhere. But many surveys have been done throughout the U.S. that have confirmed that higher education reduces rates of recidivism far more than could be due to chance, and far more effectively than any other single program. As a follow-up to our own study, we discovered that, finally, some thirty years after the first inmates were graduated, two have been returned to prison. That is less than a one per cent recidivism rate over a thirty-year period—which compares to national recidivism rates of 65 per cent within three years of leaving prison.

Strictly speaking, free higher education for inmates is an example of what would be called tertiary, not primary, prevention of violence. But I am discussing it in this chapter because I believe the principle it illustrates is relevant to the entire population, not just those who have already become violent.

Where Do We Go From Here?

A century and a half ago, we discovered that cleaning up the water supply and the sewer system was far more effective in preventing physical disease than all the doctors, medicines and hospitals in the world. What we need to learn during the coming century is that cleaning up our social and economic system, by reducing the shame-provoking inequities in social and economic status, will do far more to prevent physical violence than all the police, prisons and punishments in the world, all the prison psychiatrists we could possibly hire, and all the armies, armaments, and Armageddons we could mobilize!

What is at issue here is relative poverty, not absolute poverty. Inferiority is a relative concept. When everyone is poor together, there is no shame in being poor. As Marx said, it is not living in a hovel that causes people to feel ashamed, it is living in a hovel next to a palace. And as he also said, shame is the emotion of revolution, i.e. of violence. But one does not have to be a Marxist, or subscribe to everything he said (and I do not), in order to see how correct his insight was. Adam Smith, Amartya Sen and other non-Marxist economists have seen the same things. In his latest book, Professor Sen in *Development as Freedom* (1999) emphasized how profound the psychological injuries are that are caused by unemployment and by relative poverty. These do not merely cause economic damage to people, they also wound them emotionally. "Among its manifold effects," he points out, "unemployment contributes to social exclusion. . . , to losses of self-reliance, self-confidence, and psychological and physical health." And he reminds us that Adam Smith saw that economic inequality—relative deprivation in terms of income and wealth—can cause absolute deprivation when it exposes people to crippling and disabling intensities of shame. For example, he quotes Smith's comment that leather shoes are not a physical necessity, but they can be a social and psychological one—since anyone would be ashamed to appear in public without them. No one who has seen violent teenagers who will kill each other over a pair of sneakers, as I have, can doubt the importance and validity of what Professor Sen and Adam Smith are talking about. Shakespeare also saw the difference between absolute and relative deprivation, and how devastating the latter can be to a person's sense of his basic human dignity, when he has Lear cry:

> O, reason not the need! our basest beggars
> Are in the poorest thing superfluous.
> Allow not nature more than nature needs,
> Man's life is cheap as beast's.
>
> (II. iv. 264–67)

But how can we go about eliminating relative poverty? Clearly, education is relevant and important, and making it freely available to everyone can only help. But that alone will not solve the problem. I say that because I have worked with the most violent criminals our society produces, and I have heard politicians like John Major in the U.K. and his counterparts in the U.S. say that what we need to do to solve the problem of crime and violence is to teach criminals to learn the difference between right and wrong. In other words, we need to teach them to recognize the difference between justice and injustice, and to pursue the former and eschew the latter. But what the politicians who mouth these sentiments do not realize is that the violent criminals are perfectly aware of the difference between right and wrong, and justice and injustice. They realize that they have been victims of injustice (most of all, from those who preach to them most loudly about it), and they commit their crimes in order to achieve some measure of justice, by taking something back from a society that has subjected them to a degree of deprivation to which it does not subject others. For example, how can we, as a society, say that we have something to teach about justice, when we permit the perpetuation of an economic system in which some people inherit millions of pounds while most people inherit nothing? How can we speak of equality of opportunity under those conditions?

Violent criminals are not violent because they are dumb, out of touch with reality, or unable to recognize hypocrisy, dishonesty, and injustice when they see it. They are violent precisely because they are aware of the hypocrisy, dishonesty, and injustice that surrounds them and of which they have been the victims. That does not mean that they respond to those conditions in a rational or just way, or that we should tolerate and permit their violence—which affects their fellow victims much more often than it does their oppressors. But it does mean that we cannot expect to stop the kind of violence that we call crime until we stop the kind of violence that I have called structural in "Structural Violence" (1999). By this I mean the deaths and disabilities that are caused by the economic structure of our society, its division into rich and poor. Structural violence is not only the main *form* of violence, in the sense that poverty kills far more people (almost all of them very poor) than all the behavioral violence put together, it is also the main *cause* of violent behavior. Eliminating structural violence means eliminating relative poverty.

So how can we do that? There is an old saying that the cure for poverty is money. Since there are two forms of relative poverty—inequities in wealth and in income—we will need to deal with both. Inequities in wealth can be dealt with during the lifetimes of the wealthy by means of a wealth tax, and after their lifetimes, by means of an inheritance or estate tax, with the proceeds in either case distributed to those with less wealth. Inequities in income can be dealt with by means of a negative income tax, in which people whose incomes are below the cut-off point pay no taxes but instead receive money from the taxes paid by those with higher incomes. This strategy has been utilized on a small scale in the U.S., where it has been described by some scholars as being one of the most effective anti-poverty programs in U.S. history (along with the social security system that has lifted many of the elderly and disabled out of poverty). It has several advantages over more traditional welfare systems, of which the one most relevant to our discussion is that it spares the recipients from the humiliation often attendant on visits to welfare offices.

My point here is not that these are the only or even necessarily the best ways to alleviate the inequities in income and wealth that create feelings of injustice, envy, inferiority, and hostility, but simply to point out that there are ways to do it, they have been tried, and some of them seem to work. In principle, there is no limit to the degree to which income and wealth could be equalized. The degree to which we choose to equalize them could be decided on in part by another principle, which is that the more they were equalized, the lower the level of violence we could expect as a result. Ultimately, then, we would be left with the same question with which we started this discussion: how seriously and completely do we want to prevent violence, and how high a price are we willing to pay in order to do so? The choice is ours.

There would, of course, be many objections to such a plan, especially from the wealthy. But there is one objection that might be worth discussing here, namely, that the more we equalized income and wealth, the more we would destroy people's incentives to work. That is an argument which, if you examine it more closely, is applied only to the poor, not to the rich. The traditional defense of class stratification and the existence of a "leisure class," ever since the rise of civilization, from both Plato and Aristotle as well as from more recent social thinkers, is that a leisure class is needed in order to have the time and energy for the specialized intellectual development and technological skills that are necessary preconditions for civilization; and "leisure class" has always meant a group with a *guaranteed income*—i.e. those who did not have to work for a living. Implicit in this argument is the assumption (which I happen to think is correct, as I think the history and development of civilization proves) that when people are freed from the necessity to work—that is, when work is freely chosen rather than slavery or wage-slavery (i.e "work or starve"), they do not just vegetate in a state of "passivity and dependency." Rather, they engage in much more creative work. Coercion creates an incentive for "passive aggressiveness," because when overpowered and helpless there is no other way to express the minimal degree of autonomy that people need in order to maintain any semblance of self-esteem, dignity, and pride. Furthermore, when work is a means to an end—working in order to eat—then it is, in Marx's terms, "alienated" labor. Labor can only be liberated from alienation when work is an end in itself, entered into freely as the expression of spontaneous and voluntary creativity, curiosity, playfulness, initiative, and sociability—that is, the sense of solidarity with the community, the fulfillment of one's true and "essential" human nature as "social' and "political" animals, to be fulfilled and made human by their full participation in a culture.

In short, the contradiction in the old defense of class stratification is that it defends leisure for the leisure class, but not for the underclass. With reference to the underclass, leisure is said to destroy the incentive to work, leads to slothfulness and self-indulgence, and retards cognitive and moral development. When applied to the leisure class, the concept evokes an image of Plato and Aristotle, whose leisure was based on slave labor, creating the intellectual foundations of Western civilization; or patrician slave-owners like Washington and Jefferson laying the foundations of American civilization; or creative aristocrats like Count Leo Tolstoy or Bertrand, Earl Russell; or, even closer to home, of our own sons and daughters (or of ourselves, when we were young adults) being freed from the stultifying tasks of earning a living until well into our adult years so that we could study in expensive universities to gain specialized knowledge and skills.

As we enter the new millennium, perhaps it is worth reflecting on the fact that this could be a turning-point in the evolution of civilization, for our technologies have evolved to the point where there is no longer a need for an underclass of slaves, serfs, and wage-slaves. This division of society into a hierarchical order of upper and lower social classes did not exist until civilization was invented. The low level of technological development made this necessary to allow a class of specialists (mathematicians, inventors, poets, scientists, philosophers) the leisure for the creative work that is a prerequisite for the creation, maintenance, and further development of civilization. But slaves and underclasses are no longer needed in order to free up enough leisure time and energy for the elite to do work that is creative rather than alienated. Therefore we no longer need social classes and their concomitant, relative poverty and economic inequality, and their concomitant, violence. If we permit ourselves—and by ourselves I mean all of us, all human beings—to enjoy the fruits of the creative labor that has preceded us, we could create a society that would no longer need violence as the only means of rescuing self-esteem.

Implicit in this argument is the idea that money is neither a necessary incentive for creative work, nor the main incentive. The play that infants and children engage in is clearly an inborn, inherent trait of human beings. Play has been called the work that children do, the means by which they acquire the skills and knowledge that enable them to develop and mature into adults. Play has also been described, when applied to adults, as simply another name for work that one enjoys. We could use the word to refer to unalienated labor, creative work, work that is an end in itself. I believe that the wish and the need to engage in this creative work/play is only conditioned out of human beings by the alienating conditions to which the underclass and even the middle class in our society are subjected.

There is a large body of empirical research that is relevant to this. One category consists of psychological experiments, reviewed and summarized by Kohn in "Studies Find Reward" (1987) that call into question the widespread belief that money is an effective and even necessary way to motivate people. Consensus has emerged from major psychology departments throughout the U.S. (e.g. James Garbarino, then at Chicago, now at Cornell; Mark L. Lepper, at Stanford; Edward Deci and Richard Ryan, at Rochester; Teresa Amibile, at Brandeis) that creativity, interest, subjective satisfaction, persistence, and overall productivity all decline when a task is done for the sake of an external, extrinsic reward. The only sphere in which "material rewards *do* seem to be necessary" is that of the dull jobs "that make very little use of their abilities" (Ryan *Equality*, 1981). But that is precisely the type of work that is much less necessary now that technology has created robots and servomechanisms. The time may have come to ask whether the price we pay in violence and unhappiness is worth the reward of keeping some groups of people in menial jobs that we could easily do without.

Another relevant research program consists of studies investigating the degree of satisfaction or happiness that whole groups of people experience under differing conditions of income distribution. The consensus is that people located at *every* point on the status scale in the unequal income communities—whether at, above, or below the average—reported less personal happiness and subjective satisfaction than those in communities in which income was distributed equally (Furby, "Satisfaction with Outcome Distributions," 1981).

A third field of research has compared productivity in the U.S. with the relatively egalitarian welfare states of western Europe. The consensus has been that "productivity growth since World War II has been much faster in Europe than in the United States" (Schmitt, *New York Times*, 25 August 1999). But, since some would dismiss that finding as showing that it is easier to increase productivity when you start from a lower base (as did Europe after the devastation of the war), it should also be noted that more "recent data show that several European countries, including France, Germany, the Netherlands and Belgium have matched or even exceeded the United States' productivity levels." (Ibid.) And among the O.E.C.D. nations as a whole, Glyn and Miliband in *Paying for Inequality* (1994) have reported that "those with the fastest increases in productivity tend to be those with narrower income differences."

If all we were concerned about was preventing violence, it would not matter whether productivity diminished as wealth and income equalized. We would feel that preventing violence was so important that it was worth the sacrifice of some growth in overall Gross Domestic Product; at least we would all be poor together, and suffer less shame and less violence. But it is relevant, in the real world, to ask how high the price will be to society if we become more egalitarian. Violence is not all that people care about, though if it increases as much in the next century as it did in the last, preventing violence will turn out to be so important as to make all other considerations irrelevant.

The most extreme evidence for that might be the experience of the Third World countries. So as not to shame these states, they are now conventionally referred to as developing countries rather than undeveloped ones; this is little more than a cruel euphemism for many of them. The sad reality is not only that they are not developing, but are actually undeveloping, getting poorer. Is that because they are too egalitarian? On the contrary, by far the greatest degree of both economic inequity and violence in the world is found in the Third World countries, whose populations typically consist of a tiny oligarchy of extremely wealthy rulers, a vast majority of starving peasants and no middle class. In comparison, even the United States looks like a peaceful social democracy. If economic inequity were a prerequisite for economic growth, one would expect these countries to be growing by leaps and bounds. Instead they are regressing. If we look at the group as a whole, we would have to conclude that the higher the degree of economic inequity in a society, the lower its productivity and rate of overall economic growth. Unequal societies are not only the most violent; they are also the least productive.

CHAPTER 6

SECONDARY PREVENTION: EARLY INTERVENTION

The secondary prevention of physical illness consists of identifying the individuals who are at increased risk of becoming ill, such as those with high blood pressure or elevated serum cholesterol levels, and intervening to remove, diminish or neutralize the risk factor before they become ill. Exactly the same principles apply to the secondary prevention of violence. In this chapter I will briefly summarize a variety of such programs that have been adopted and found to be effective.

Secondary prevention, like primary, is more effective in absolute terms and also more cost-effective (more benefits per money spent) than punishment after people have already committed an act of serious violence. Even more importantly, the most significant help we can give victims is to prevent their being victimized in the first place. This is partly why it is so important to shift the emphasis of our public investments concerning violence away from our current wasteful and ineffective over-emphasis on police, prisons, and punishments, and toward early intervention before people have become violent.

Some of the most rigorous research on the secondary prevention of violence has been conducted by the RAND Corporation in California (Greenwood, et al., *Diverting Children from a Life of Crime*, 1996). For example, they have been able to document the effectiveness of two programs designed to prevent the development of future violence in a demographic group that was, statistically, at increased risk—children of mothers who were young, single, and poor. The first program consisted of training for parents and psychotherapy for families with young children who have shown aggressive behavior in school. The second was a program of providing cash and other incentives to induce disadvantaged high school students to graduate. They then compared the arrest rates of these children over the years as they grew up with those of control groups that had the same demographic characteristics, in order to calculate how many crimes the interventions had succeeded in averting. Finally, they compared the effectiveness of those programs with that of the "three-strikes" law in California, which mandates a life sentence in prison for anyone who is convicted of a third felony. What they concluded was that the two prevention programs reduced the crime rate by approximately the same amount that the three-strikes law had (about 20 per cent), but at only about one-sixth of the cost—and, of course, without having to imprison anyone. That brings us to another extremely important method of secondary prevention—governmentally provided support for parents with young children. One of the most powerful reasons that being born to a single mother in the United States leads to higher arrest rates later in life is because that family situation is so likely to be associated with poverty. For example, in the U.S. in 1994, 59 per cent of children in single-parent families were living, and all too often dying, in relative poverty, as compared with only 13 per cent of those living with two parents. (Relative poverty is defined, in this study, as having 50 per cent or less of the national median adjusted disposable personal income, which includes the benefits received from government welfare programs.) That neither of those levels of child poverty is necessary can be seen by the fact that the U.S. rate of poverty among single-parent children is exactly twice as high as the average among 14 countries of western Europe (including the U.K.), where it is 29 per cent. For that matter, the U.S. rate of poverty among two-parent families is also almost twice as high as it is in western Europe: 13 per cent versus 7.5 per cent. Why is this? One major reason is because virtually every western European country provides family allowances for families with children, whether they have one or two parents. The effect of this policy, and of all the other governmental redistribution programs, is that the European social democracies succeed in reducing the rates of relative poverty among children by an average of 48 per cent (from what it would be without these programs), whereas the U.S. reduces child poverty rates by only 13 per cent (Smeeding, "Financial Poverty in Developed Countries," 1997).

Pre-school educational programs, such as "Head Start" and the Perry pre-school program, have also been shown to reduce later delinquency and crime, as well as having many other desirable effects. Some studies have indicated that tax-payers save four dollars for every one spent on such programs because the rates of future arrests, imprisonment, unemployment, welfare dependency, and so on are so much lower among those who have attended pre-school programs.

Once children are in school, programs teaching them how to resolve conflicts peacefully appear to reduce the rate of future violence (Prothrow-Stith, *Deadly Consequences*, 1993). And despite the fact that some politicians apparently believed that the high-risk youths who live in the poverty-stricken inner-city ghettos were beyond salvation, and therefore ridiculed the provision of supervised after-school recreational activities as so much "midnight basketball"—implying that they were a waste of tax-payers' money—the fact is that such programs have been among the most dramatically successful in reducing the rates of teenage crime and violence. Most criminal behavior among school-age youth occurs, not surprisingly, in the hours following the end of the school day (from 3 p.m. on). So targeting those hours as the time to provide supervised activities, coaching, and teaching in sports, music, art, drama, and so on, was not only logical, it has also been successful.

Children who witness violence in their families or neighborhoods are also at increased risk of becoming violent themselves. In order to prevent this from happening, a group of child psychiatrists and psychoanalysts at the Child Study Center at Yale University, under the leadership of Donald Cohen and Steven Marans have entered into a partnership with the New Haven Police Department, under the terms of which the police notify the Center whenever a violent or traumatic incident has occurred to which a child was exposed—day or night. When that happens, a member of the Center staff immediately goes to the site of the incident, interviews the child and other family members, and arranges for follow-up consultations and interventions as needed (*The Police–Mental Health Partnership*, 1995). The program is still being developed, and it will be some time before it is possible to evaluate its success, but it certainly exemplifies a logical and innovative response to a type of situation that is well known to predict future violence.

That program also exemplifies another innovative development in violence prevention which the New Haven police were among the first to implement, called "community policing"—i.e. training and encouraging police officers to develop ongoing relationships with the neighborhood residents for whom they work, getting to know their problems, and learning how to help solve them proactively, rather than simply waiting for a crime to occur and then reacting by arresting someone. This approach has been followed by declining crime rates in a number of different cities in which it has been tried. What is notable about it is that it redefines the professional role of the police officer so as to incorporate many elements of what traditionally has been called social work—or community psychiatry. And it appears to be much more successful than traditional police practices.

Child abuse is another well known cause of increased risk of future violence. Two responses are important in order to reduce this risk: preventing the child abuse itself, and, where that has not been possible, intervening so as to help children exposed to this type of trauma recover from it without going on to become violent themselves. Most developed nations have child-abuse notification systems that mandate reporting to a central registry whenever doctors, teachers, or other adults become aware of a case of child abuse or have reason to suspect it. While child abuse itself has not disappeared as a result—on the contrary, the number of reported and substantiated cases has increased over the years, at least in the United States—the number of cases of *fatal* child abuse have declined by 50 per cent; so it seems that the system is helping at least in that important respect. In fact, both the reporting system and the widespread public education that is part of it have probably played a major part in that decline.

But of course merely reporting child abuse after it has occurred is not as desirable as preventing it. In that regard, it is relevant to know that fatal child abuse is *sixty* times more common in families with incomes under $15,000 than it is in those with incomes over $30,000!

(Sedlock and Broadhurst, *Third National Incidence Study of Child Abuse and Neglect*, 1996.) And virtually every other variety of child abuse appears to be much more common in the poorer families than in the more affluent. So in this context also, diminishing the inequity in incomes could be one of the most powerful means of preventing violence. Providing home visits from nurses, social workers, etc., to mothers who are at increased risk of abusing their children—single, poor teenage mothers—to help them learn how to understand and raise their children, has also been shown to bring about significant decreases in the rate of child abuse.

Mothers who have been abused in the past or are currently being beaten by their husbands or boyfriends are also at increased risk of abusing their children; therefore providing them with counseling, psychotherapy, treatment for post-traumatic stress, or access to a shelter for battered women, can help the mother and also decrease the likelihood of her becoming violent toward her child.

Drugs and Violence

The last risk factor predicting increased likelihood of violent behavior is substance abuse. However, the reason for that correlation is widely misunderstood to mean that illicit drugs themselves cause violent behavior through their psychopharmacological effects on brain and behavior. In fact, the opposite is true. (Miczek, et al., "Alcohol, Drugs of Abuse, Aggression and Violence," in Reiss and Roth *Understanding and Preventing Violence*, 1994.) Two of the most widely used illicit drugs actually inhibit, or prevent, violence. Their names are marijuana and heroin (and the other opiates). People under the influence of these drugs are actually less likely to engage in violent behavior, under otherwise identical conditions, than people who are not under their influence. The effect of the stimulant drugs, cocaine and the amphetamines, on violent behavior is more complicated, but can be summed up by saying that they stimulate violence in some people, especially those with pre-existing borderline psychotic personality disorders who may become paranoid under the influence of these drugs; inhibit it in others, such as children and young people with attention-deficit disorder with hyperactivity, and other problems; and have no discernible effect one way or the other on violent behavior for most people. And violence is not really a significant part of the problems created by the hallucinogenic drugs, such as LSD or mescaline, nor do they cause a significant amount of the violence associated with drug use.

Most of the violence associated with the use of the illegal drugs is caused by the fact that the drugs have been made illegal—as a result of which their economic value has been greatly enhanced, one could even say subsidized, by the government. There is an enormous and extraordinarily lucrative market in these drugs, which, since they are illegal, cannot be regulated in the normal, peaceful way that markets for legal commodities are regulated, that is, by the government. As a result of this, the drug dealers engage in extremely violent wars with each other to gain control over as much of the market as they can. That is what causes the vast majority of the violence associated with illegal drugs. The drugs themselves are not causing the violence. The legal system is causing it. The "War on Drugs" is causing it—by precipitating "drug wars" between the drug dealers. That is why the most effective way to prevent the violence associated with the use of illegal drugs would be to treat them as a problem in public health and preventive medicine (which they are), and provide treatment for those who are addicted to them, and stop treating them as a criminal problem. Most of the violence associated with the illegal drugs would end tomorrow—the Colombian drug cartel and the inner city drug gangs would go out of business—if we decriminalized those drugs today.

Ironically, the only drug that has been shown to stimulate violent behavior, through its psychopharmacological effects on brain and behavior, is one that is legal—alcohol. And the most dangerous drug of all, without any close competitors—the drug whose very use is an act of violence, since it kills both those who use it and those whom they expose to it, and kills incomparably more people than are killed in the gang wars precipitated by the illegal drugs—is another legal drug, tobacco. So the net effect of the drug laws has been to outlaw the drugs that prevent violence, legalize the one that causes violence, legalize the other one whose use is an act of violence, precipitate violence over the sale of the illegal (but violence-preventing) drugs, subsidize an illegal drug industry which as a result is powerful enough to destabilize several fragile Third World countries, exacerbate the AIDS epidemic, and so on. Clearly, repealing these laws and providing treatment rather than punishment would be one of the most important and effective steps we could take in the secondary prevention of violence. The RAND Corporation (Caulkins, et al., *Mandatory Minimum Drug Sentences*, 1997), for example, found that treatment of heavy users of drugs reduced serious crimes against both persons and property ten times as much as conventional law enforcement did, and fifteen times as much as mandatory minimum sentences. And, not surprisingly, treatment was also vastly more effective in reducing cocaine consumption than either conventional law enforcement or mandatory minimum sentences.

CHAPTER 7

TERTIARY PREVENTION: THERAPEUTIC INTERVENTION

Ironically, despite the fact that everyone is familiar with the cliché that an ounce of prevention is worth a pound of cure, when most of us think of medicine we usually think of the cure, or treatment, of established diseases, even though of the three levels of fighting disease this is the least important and effective—that is, the least cost-effective, in relative terms, *and* the least clinically effective, in absolute terms. Exactly the same is true of discussions of violence prevention in the mass media and the political arena, most of which focus on courts, police, prisons, and punishment as the major tools for fighting crime and violence, even though they are far less effective in reducing the rates of serious violence, in both relative and absolute terms, than primary and secondary prevention. As I will argue, the burden of proof lies with anyone who claims to show that prisons and punishments reduce the overall levels of violence at all; a great deal of evidence suggests that they may actually increase violence in a society. Police forces have only improved their ability to prevent violence to the extent that they have begun focusing on prevention before crimes occur rather than on punishments after they do, as in the concept of "community policing" to which I referred in the last chapter—the shift away from tertiary and toward primary and secondary prevention.

I am not denying that both clinical medicine and the criminal justice and penal systems will presumably always have a role to play in protecting the public health and safety, since even primary and secondary prevention can never be completely successful. My point is simply that it should be a distinctly tertiary role. The most common mistake that has been made in both the healthcare system and the criminal justice system in the United States has been to give the primary role, in terms of our investments of time and money, to tertiary prevention, and to give the tertiary role to primary prevention. This costs more in the long run, and achieves less.

The tertiary prevention of violence is pursued in the criminal courts and the system of police, prisons and punishments. I say "pursued" rather than "achieved" because tertiary prevention is not usually successful in preventing the spread of violence. Even that may be too mild a conclusion. Like the physicians delivering babies in Vienna in the 1840s, who, as their colleague Semmelweiss showed, were inadvertently infecting their patients with "puerperal fever," most of the practices of the criminal justice and penal systems actually increase the rates of violence in a society rather than decreasing them, regardless of how well-meaning individual practitioners in that system may be. In that sense, the criminal justice and penal systems are at about the same level of development in their efforts to fight violence today as obstetric medicine was at the time of Semmelweiss. We now know what the mistake was that those obstetricians were making: they were not washing their hands or sterilizing their equipment. What is the mistake the criminal justice system is making? The major mistake, I believe, is the failure to differentiate between restraint and punishment; and to imagine that punishment will prevent, or deter, violence. Does it? Let us examine the evidence.

1 If we review the past sixty years of research on child-rearing, we find that the most solidly confirmed and consistent finding is that the more severely children are punished, the more violent they become, both during childhood and after they become adults.

2 The violent criminals with whom I worked for 25 years had been punished by their parents as severely as it is possible to punish someone without actually killing him. In fact, the most violent among them were those who had been most severely punished—the survivors of attempted murder, usually at the hands of a parent. If punishment deterred violence, these men would never have become violent in the first place.

3 On a day-to-day basis in the prison I saw the effects of punishment. The more severely the prisoners were punished by the prison officers

the more violent they would become, and the more violent they became, the more severely they would be punished, in an endless, mutually self-defeating vicious circle that routinely culminated in the inmate's becoming so enraged that he stopped caring whether he lived or died, as long as he could get revenge on those he saw as tormenting him.

The criminal justice and penal systems have been operating on the basis of a huge mistake, namely, the belief that punishment will deter, prevent, or inhibit violence, when in fact it is the most powerful stimulus of violence that we have yet discovered. And that can be understood in terms of the psychodynamics of violent behavior as I summarized them in earlier chapters: punishment increases feelings of shame and humiliation, and decreases feelings of guilt; and those are exactly the psychological conditions that give rise to violent behavior, in which the rage that has been provoked by being humiliated is not inhibited by feelings of guilt.

What then can we do about crime and punishment? To ask that question is to ask what we can do about *violence*—whether it takes the form of crime *or* punishment. The first and most important principle might be to start doing nothing, or in other words, to stop doing the things that we are already doing that only stimulate violence—such as responding to the kind of violence that we call crime with the kind that we call punishment.

I am not suggesting that it would make sense to let those who are actively raping and murdering others walk the streets. Physical *restraint* of those who are currently and actively physically violent, including confining or "quarantining" them in a locked facility, is at times the only way, in our ignorance, we have yet discovered to prevent further violence, temporarily. But to *punish* people—that is, to deliberately cause them pain—above and beyond the degree that is unavoidable in the act of *restraining* them, only *constitutes* further violence (on our part), and only *causes* further violence (on the part of the "criminals" we punish).

And since restraint itself unavoidably involves coercion and physical force, and will inevitably be experienced by some (though not all) as a form of punishment, it would make sense to utilize it only for those who are physically violent themselves. In other words, it is time that we stopped overcrowding our prisons, distorting our economic priorities, and subjecting the non-violent to violence and teaching them to become violent themselves by placing *anyone* in prison for a *non-violent* crime. To use our prisons for those who have committed only crimes against property, or drug offenses, or have offended against someone's sense of morality, as with prostitution or gambling, is self-defeating if our goal is to decrease the amount of violence in our society; for *the most effective way to turn a non-violent person into a violent one is to send him to prison.* This does not always work, of course, as is shown by the examples of Thoreau, Gandhi, Martin Luther King, Nelson Mandela, and others who have survived the violence of imprisonment without becoming violent themselves. But of course the mass of men who are sent to prison for non-violent offenses are not sent there for engaging in principled political protests; they are sent there for minor (often victimless) crimes born of weakness, poverty, and despair, such as drug addiction or (in the case of women) prostitution; and even though they may not have harmed anyone, most of them do not have the personal strength or the moral resources of a King or a Mandela. I have seen far too many of them who have concluded that the best defense (against being brutalized by their guards and their fellow inmates) was a violent offense—a strategy they carried with them onto the streets after they were released from prison.

Why We Need Anti-Prisons

Prisons themselves could actually start preventing violence, rather than stimulating it, if we took everyone out of them, demolished the buildings, and replaced them with a new and different kind of institution—namely, a locked, secure residential college, whose purpose and functions would be educational and therapeutic, not punitive. It would make sense to organize such a facility as a therapeutic community, with a full range of treatments for substance abuse and any other medical and mental health services needed to help the individual heal the damage that deformed his character and stunted his humanity.

If it seems utopian to replace prisons with schools, let me remind you that *prisons already are schools and always have been*—except that they are schools in crime and violence, in humiliation, degradation, brutalization and exploitation, not in peace and love and dignity. *I am merely suggesting that we replace one already existing type of school with another.*

Such a program would enable those who have been violent to adopt non-violent means for developing the feelings of self-esteem and self-respect, for being respected by others, and of being able to take legitimate and realistic pride in their skills and knowledge and achievements, which all human beings need if they are to be able to find alternatives to violent behavior when their self-esteem is threatened. It would also enable them to become employable and self-sufficient, and to make a productive contribution to society when they return to the community. But *before that can happen, we will have to renounce our own urge to engage in violence—that is, punishment*—and decide that we want to engage in educational and therapeutic endeavors instead, so as to facilitate maturation, development, and healing.

What programs would a prison need to utilize in order to maximize the likelihood that the people sent to it would renounce violence as a behavioral strategy? To begin with, it would need to be an anti-prison. Beginning with its architecture, it would need to convey an entirely different message. Current prisons are modeled architecturally after zoos—or rather, after the kinds of zoos that used to exist, but that have been replaced with zoological parks because the animals' keepers began to realize that the old zoos, with concrete floors and walls and steel bars were too inhumane for animals to survive in. Yet we still keep our human animals in zoos that no humane society would permit for animals. And the architecture itself conveys that message to the prisoners: "You are an animal, for this is a zoo, and zoos are what animals are put in." And then we act surprised when the men and women we treat that way actually behave like animals, both when they are in this human zoo and after they return to the community.

So we would need to build an anti-prison that would actually look as if it had been built for human beings rather than animals, i.e. that was as home-like and pleasant and civilized and humane as possible. Once we had done that, we could offer those who had been sent there the opportunity to acquire as much education and/or vocational training as they had the ability and energy and interest to obtain. We would of course need to provide treatment for whatever medical, dental, psychiatric, or substance-abuse problems they had, and would want to incorporate many of the principles of a therapeutic community into the everyday routines of this residential school, with frequent group discussions with the other residents and staff members with training in psychotherapy. The goal would be to replace the "monster factories" that most prisons now are with therapeutic communities designed to enable people who are deeply damaged, and damaging, to recover their humanity or to gain a degree of humanity they had never been able to acquire; in short, to help them heal themselves and learn, in the process, how to heal others and even repair some of the damage they have done. This is obviously a huge question, but I will attempt here to summarize a few of the basic principles that governed the way we were able to bring about a dramatic reduction in the amount of violence in two correctional settings, beginning with the Massachusetts prisons between 1981 and 1991, and then continuing with a discussion of the San Francisco jails from 1998 to the present.

Violence Prevention Workshops

The first principle may seem almost too obvious to mention, but prisons are such abnormal, violent, pathogenic, traumatizing, brutalizing, and dehumanizing environments, both for inmates and staff, that I learned that I had to emphasize the obvious right from the start: namely, the foundation on which all relationships must be based, if they are going to be able to lead away from violence rather than toward it, is an attitude of genuine, mutual respect. One takes this for granted in any other setting, personal, professional, or psychotherapeutic. But in prisons nothing normal or human can be taken for granted, and when I speak of the importance of treating people with respect I am not talking about anything that is necessarily very subtle; I am talking about avoiding the attitude of the new prison guard who announced my arrival on a cell-block to interview a prisoner one day by yelling at the top of his voice, "Hey shit-head, the nut-doctor's here to see you!" Of course, the older and wiser guards knew better, and would attempt to teach their younger colleagues how seriously they were endangering everybody by behaving that way, just as I would try to teach the junior staff members I was supervising that if they could not genuinely treat each of the violent men they would be interviewing with respect, making sure never to violate their basic human dignity, they had better find somewhere else to work, because it would not be safe for them or any of the rest of us, nor would it be helpful for the prisoners. This actually incorporates two principles:

1 By treating everyone with respect, you teach them to treat everyone with respect also, because the only effective teaching is by example.

2 Just as the most powerful provocation to violent behavior is disrespect, the most powerful means of preventing violence is universal respect.

But how can one *respect* people who have been as cruel and destructive toward other people as these violent criminals have been? By discovering, or helping to foster, some part of their personality that is not cruel and destructive, some part of them that would like to stop being violent. They are likely to find that this is the part they are most frightened of, since it is the one most unwilling to engage in the violent defenses against the threat of humiliation so overwhelming as to threaten the cohesion and the survival of their personality. By analogy, in every psychotic patient there is a part of the mind that is rational and in touch with reality, and that is the part that a therapist can work with. Likewise, with every sociopathic or narcissistic violent criminal there is, or there will be (if one is persistent and patient enough), a part of the personality that is capable of feeling empathy and concern, guilt and remorse, toward the people they victimized, though they will try to conceal or run away from that side of themselves.

Just as you do not have to judge someone by the worst thing he ever did, so you do not have to reduce someone's whole personality to its most destructive or pathological set of defenses. Of course you have to recognize those for what they are, if you are going to be able to help someone outgrow them; but if that is all you work with, you are neglecting to foster whatever healthier and more mature potential the person may have.

I can understand why some might ask why we should expend so much energy on people who have done such terrible things; why shouldn't we work instead with troubled youth in the community, for example, before they become as destructive and violent as these men? I can only answer that by saying, first, that this is not an either/or choice; of course we should also work with people before they become as damaged as these men. But there are some things about the causes and prevention of violence that we can learn only by working with those "dead souls" who are the most violent people of all—just as there are some things we can learn about the physical diseases that kill people only by examining their bodies after they have died. The lessons we learn from the prison population can turn out to be helpful and even necessary if we want to be able to learn how to help people in the community who are not (yet) so damaged. And the extremely violent men who are in the prisons are still alive. Some of them, even some who have been very violent, will be returned to the community by the legal system, so it can make a great deal of difference to the safety of the public what kind of treatment they have received while they were incarcerated. And even those who remain in the prisons can still be dangerous, to prison staff members, visitors, other prisoners, and themselves, except insofar as we can help to reverse that condition. And there is one all-important difference between those whose bodies have died and those who have suffered the death of the soul: the latter can be resurrected, at least to the degree that they will not remain violent toward anyone.

After thirty years of working with the most violent men our society produces, I am convinced that we do not need to give up on anyone. Even the most intractably violent people can learn to live with others in ways that are constructive rather than destructive. So there are many reasons why even those who feel nothing but detestation for every violent criminal in the world might still conclude, on the basis of self-interest, that these men deserve all the attention we can give them.

That leads to another meaning of the concept of respect. The German word for attention—*Achtung*—also means respect. And that makes sense: the way you truly respect someone is to pay attention to them, and if you are not giving them your full attention, you are disrespecting them. That is one reason, I think, that psychotherapy and psychoanalysis are such deep forms of respect for human beings and human dignity. They involve, indeed they consist of, paying full attention to another human being. It is not only Willie Loman in *Death of a Salesman* to whom attention must be paid; we all need attention. When we get it, we know that we are being respected. That also helps to explain the etiology of violence: assaulting people is a foolproof way to get their attention. Since everyone needs respect/attention, if they cannot get it non-violently, they will get it violently. And I have never met a group of people who had been so profoundly neglected and deprived, and who had received so little of either attention or respect, as the prison inmates.

It is ironic, or worse, self-defeating, and even tragic, that the whole purpose of prisons, the attitudes and message that are expressed symbolically by the concrete actions and concrete buildings of the penal system, from their architecture (completely enclosed) to their geographic siting (as far from the community as possible) to their security apparatus and sentencing procedures ("Lock them up and throw away the key") can be seen as a massive and extraordinarily expensive way to achieve one purpose: namely, to *avoid* paying attention to those in prison. That underlying principle is even more fully expressed in those prisons-within-the-prisons, their solitary confinement units, and the ultimate refinement, the last possible step in this direction, beyond which it is hard to imagine that even the most elaborate human technology could go, the so-called "supermax" prison, in which the *entire* prison consists of nothing but solitary confinement cells, and everything is designed so that inmates, as far as possible, will have no direct physical or even visual contact with (or receive attention from) any single living, breathing human being for years at a time! Thirty states within the United States have in recent years built these bizarre inventions, which as of January 2000 held an estimated 25,000 prisoners in universal permanent isolation—a development for which the U.S. was roundly condemned by the United Nations Committee Against Torture in May 2000.

A report by the American Friends Service Committee (*Inside the Walls*, 2000) noted, "While other countries do operate isolation units, their use is far more restricted. In the United Kingdom, for example, 0.1 per cent of the prison population is confined in administrative segregation, as compared to 1.8 per cent of the U.S. prison population that is held in supermax prisons, and an unknown number of people in isolation units within traditional prisons and jails." But even that underestimates the difference between the U.S. and almost every other nation. Our imprisonment rate is six to ten times greater than that of any other country except two former police states, Russia and South Africa.

A related principle for preventing violence is this: always give people a chance to talk, remembering that *the only alternative to action —including violent action—is words.* This is always true in general, but it can be a matter of life and death in hostage negotiations. On a much larger scale, this is why negotiations are often the only alternative to war. It is also why freedom of speech and of the press are powerful means of preventing violence for societies as a whole. Finally, on a microcosmic scale, this is one reason why psychotherapy is so important a tool for preventing violence—the whole point of it is to help people express their feelings by means of words rather than fists or weapons; to get what they want by verbal requests or negotiations rather than with fists or weapons; and to learn to understand themselves, be aware of themselves, and able to reflect on, assess, criticize, and reconsider their actions by means of words and thoughts, rather than going through life thoughtlessly and unconsciously.

Another important therapeutic principle in work with violent prisoners has already been mentioned: never forget the difference between *punishment* and *restraint.* By punishment I mean the deliberate infliction of pain on a person above and beyond any that is unavoidable in the course of restraining him from harming anyone. Always remember that:

1 Punishment stimulates violence.
2 Punishment is itself a form of violence.
3 Violence only leads to more violence.
4 Punishment is just another word for revenge.
5 Revenge is endless, leading only to endless vicious circles of counter-revenge.

Restraint, by contrast—limiting a person's freedom when that is the only way to prevent him from harming himself or others, but doing so without inflicting any avoidable physical or psychological pain or injury—may be the only way to prevent violence when the person does not respond to words. In fact, providing restraint when a person is not controlling his violent impulses (but only for so long as he needs it in order to avoid harming anyone) can be reassuring and supportive, a sign of caring, and failure to provide it can leave the person who lacks self-control feeling overwhelmed, panicky, unloved, and unsafe. If a parent or teacher allows one child to be violent toward another, the violent child can only be worried that the adult will allow someone to hurt him as well if he gets in a fight with someone who is stronger than he is. There is no reason to think that the psychology of adults differs from that of children in this respect. People of all ages can only feel safe when the rules of the group are that no one is allowed to harm anyone. And I learned a long time ago, in my first year of psychiatric training, that violent people are most afraid of losing control of their own violent impulses. When I was the psychiatrist-on-call one night in one of the psychiatric teaching hospitals at the Harvard Medical School, I was paged to go to one of the in-patient wards to help the nursing staff deal with a patient who was keeping a large group of nurses, orderlies and security personnel at bay by holding a chair over his head and threatening everyone with mayhem if they came near him. I knew he was paranoid, so I began by trying to reassure him that no one was going to harm him. That got nowhere.

Finally, I looked around, noticed how many staff members were in the room, and reassured him that there were so many people there that they could make sure that he would not be able to hurt anyone. After digesting that thought, he looked relieved, put down the chair, agreed to take his medication, and went back to his room to go to sleep.

I then frequently found myself confronted with the same issue once I started directing mental health programs in prisons. On an almost daily basis, one prisoner or another would ask us to lock him in his cell because he was afraid that he was going to "go off" (prison slang for lose his temper or even go berserk and lose control completely). What they seemed to fear, even more than that they would hurt someone or get hurt or in trouble themselves, was the sensation of being completely out of control of their own impulses, which seemed to induce a kind of panic, a sensation of, in effect, losing their minds. We told them that we would agree to lock them up for as long as they felt they needed it, but in the meantime we would talk with them about what had precipitated the problem, and attempt to help them regain the sense of being in control of themselves so they would not need the external controls that we were supplying.

One implication of this is that therapy is only possible when both parties involved, the patient and the therapist, feel physically safe and in control. We went out of our way to make sure that there was adequate security available when we were meeting with someone who appeared to us to be potentially dangerous, such as by installing "panic buttons" on each desk so that we could call for help if attacked, or asking a correction officer to remain in the vicinity in case of need. And as I said, the prisoners also felt more secure when it was clear that there was adequate security and safety in the environment.

Conversely, when people experience restraint as a punishment, rather than as a helpful or reassuring alternative to punishment, it is essential to remember that depriving a person of the freedom to hurt anyone is as much "punishment" as we ever need in order to prevent violence and keep everyone safe. As a great British criminologist, Sir Alexander Paterson, said, offenders are sent to prison "as a punishment, not *for* punishment"—though restraint provided in an atmosphere of universal respect for human beings and human life can also provide what a great British psychoanalyst, D. W. Winnicott, called a secure holding environment, and failure to provide that when it is the only way to prevent violence can be a much worse punishment than providing it.

Finally, *assuring access to education and employment is one of the most powerful, effective and successful means for preventing violence,* as well as one of the most inexpensive and cost-effective. Nothing that we can provide for our imprisoned violent criminals can contribute more than this to the safety of the public, the rehabilitation of the prisoners, and savings to the taxpayer.

In recent years the Sheriff of San Francisco, Michael Hennessey, together with the Assistant Sheriff, Michael Marcum, and their Program Administrator, Sunny Schwartz, have been making a concerted effort to develop an experimental, intensive, comprehensive violence-prevention program for men who have been sent to jail for violent crimes, and to replace retributive justice with restorative justice. For the past three years a special cell-block housing sixty-four men has been the site for this experiment, in which the men are engaged in a variety of educational, therapeutic and artistic group activities for twelve hours a day, six days a week, for as long as they are in the jail (which can range from one day to several months).

One of the components of this program is a highly structured group discussion that meets several times a week, the point of which is to deconstruct and reconstruct what the creator and designer of this activity, a community organizer and group therapist from Scotland named Hamish Sinclair, calls the "male-role belief system." The point of this is to engage the men in a process at the end of which they will have become able to identify, question, and criticize virtually every assumption and value that underlies the definition of masculinity (and femininity) in our culture, so that they can recognize and become aware not only of the assumptions and values that have been guiding their actions (and leading them into violence and into jail), but also how irrational, arbitrary, destructive, and self-destructive these assumptions and values are. For example, they learn to recognize how they have been imposing a hierarchical structure on their relationships with people, in which one person (or sex) has to be regarded as superior, and the other as inferior, the corollary of which is that unless they impose the inferior role on the other person in the relationship, then they are not only in the inferior role themselves, they have lost their masculinity, since masculinity is defined as superiority. This is a recipe for violence, of course, when other people resist being treated as inferior, as they often do. But the men not only participate in these guided group discussions, after they "graduate" from them many join an intensive training program that equips them to lead these same groups, both with other jail inmates and with people in the community. In fact, every person who goes through this special program is encouraged to participate in violence-prevention work in the community after they leave the jail.

Another activity consists of regularly scheduled group meetings with victims of violence, such as the survivors of murder victims, who tell them in often painful detail what impact their victimization has had on their lives. A third activity consists of writing and then acting in one-act plays based on their own chaotic, traumatic and violence-ridden lives, which they do both in the jail and in the community.

I have been asked to evaluate this program, so I am attempting to compare "graduates" of this program with a matched control group that is incarcerated in conventional jails. Part of the evaluation consists of comparing the frequency of violence in the experimental and the control groups, both while they are in jail and after they return to the community. In the year before the experimental program was started, there were thirty-eight serious violent incidents in the cell-block in which it is now taking place. During the first month of the new program, there was one violent incident, and for the following twelve months there were none. The cell-block housing the control group, meanwhile, continued to have three dozen violent incidents over the course of the year. The more ambitious goal of the program is, of course, to reduce violent behavior after the men leave the jail, and to assess that we will be comparing rates of violent recidivism during the first three years after men in the experimental and control groups return to the community. So far, we only have preliminary data for the first year after leaving jail, but the results are promising. It appears that men who were in the experimental program for two months had 42 per cent fewer arrests for violent crimes during the first year after leaving than the control group did; those who were in it for three months had 50 per cent fewer arrests; and those who had been in for four months or more had 80 per cent fewer arrests. All in all, this program would seem to support the hypothesis that violence can be prevented, and that a radical transformation of penal policies and practices may be the most effective, and perhaps the only effective, way to accomplish that goal, for those who have already become violent and been incarcerated.

Conjugal Visits and Furloughs

If we wanted our anti-prison to be as effective as possible in preventing violence, we would allow prisoners to have conjugal visits, in a setting of privacy. Many studies have found that the level of violence that prisoners show, both while they are in prison and after they return to the community, is significantly lower if they have been able to have conjugal visits. For the same reason, and because it has also been shown to reduce violent behavior during and after imprisonment, we would provide the opportunity for the residents who had shown themselves reasonably responsible and reliable and stable, to have temporary visits, or "furloughs," to their homes. We would enable them to leave this locked residential school and return to their homes as soon as they had demonstrated that they had developed alternatives to violence as the means of expressing themselves and getting what they wanted. After they had left, we would want to provide after-care services and support of as comprehensive a nature as they needed to help them make the transition back into the community, including help in getting further education or obtaining employment, follow-up treatment for substance abuse and/or mental illness. By providing as many of them as possible with the necessary training and supervision, they could in turn become violence-prevention counselors themselves, working with youth groups or other community agencies.

It goes without saying that such a remodeled "anti-penal" system would have no room in it for the death penalty. It is clear that *punishment stimulates violence*, and it is even more clear that *the ultimate punishment stimulates ultimate violence.*

Alternative Sentencing Models

Finally, a system that would be as effective as possible in achieving the tertiary prevention of violence would use alternatives to incarceration to the greatest extent that would be compatible with the safety of the individual and the community, i.e. with those who were currently able and willing to renounce the use of violence. Many judges today, recognizing the profound psychological impact that every step of the criminal justice process, from arrest to sentencing and post-release planning, can have on those who come before the courts as defendants, are developing a new approach to their role called therapeutic jurisprudence. As a consequence, a new flexibility in sentencing practices is gradually evolving as the purpose of the criminal justice system becomes reoriented more toward therapy and away from punishment and revenge. (A complete bibliography of scholarship on this subject can be found at http://www.law.arizona.edu/upr-intj.)

Many courts and correctional administrators are also replacing the approach based on retributive justice with one based on restorative or reparative justice, and attempting to maximize the extent to which criminal offenders can provide some meaningful restitution to their victims and to the community. "Drug courts" are being created in more and more jurisdictions, in which treatment for substance abuse is being offered in place of imprisonment and punishment.

Community service is being utilized more frequently as it is becoming increasingly obvious that simply punishing someone by putting him in prison for the sake of making him feel pain benefits no one, costs the community money, and deprives the community of service the offender could have provided if given the opportunity to stay out of prison. The use of house arrest, sometimes monitored by means of ankle bracelets, can enable many inmates to have the freedom to live at home while still providing safety for the community.

Finally, the special group of people (mostly men) who have sexually victimized children are usually quite different in personality and behavior patterns from those whose pattern is one of physical violence toward adults. Most pedophiles are non-violent, in the sense that they do not physically injure their victims (however much they may injure them psychologically). Those who are non-violent can usually be treated successfully in intensive out-patient treatment programs staffed by specially trained professionals, which they are required to participate in at least part of every day, so that there is close monitoring and follow-up. Such individuals usually need to continue to participate in these programs more or less indefinitely, but it is just as true that as long as they are participating in intensive ongoing therapy they do not need to be in prison in order for the children of the community to be safe from them. But it is also true that their participation in such treatment usually needs to be mandated by the courts as the only alternative to imprisonment, because as soon as a court order of that sort expires, many sex-offenders will drop out of treatment and become at risk of reoffending. My point in saying all this is to stress that the way the penal system deals with many such men today gives us the worst of both worlds instead of the best of both worlds: pedophiles are often deprived of their freedom to a greater extent than is needed (i.e. placed in prison) for a much shorter period than is needed (e.g. a year or two), when in fact they may not need to be locked up at all but they may need to remain in intensive, mandated out-patient treatment for a very long time.

One last question that these men pose: should they be given sex hormone treatments that reduce the strength of their sexual impulses? I have had a number of such men request these treatments, because they wanted to stop offending sexually against children (or adults) and did not feel in control of themselves. Frankly, I can see no reason to deprive a man of such treatment if he wants it and it will help (which it seems to do with most of those who use it).

CHAPTER 8

WHO BENEFITS FROM VIOLENCE?

The main obstacle to preventing violence is not lack of knowledge as to how to do it. Rather, it is lack of the political will to make the changes in our society that would prevent violence. This simple fact has been largely obscured by a great deal of political propaganda whose effect is to persuade people that policies that stimulate violence actually prevent it, and that policies that prevent it actually stimulate it. Here are a few examples of what I mean:

1 As I pointed out in Chapter 6, the main cause of the increased violence associated with illicit drugs is not the drugs themselves, it is the politicians who passed laws making the drugs illegal. If their goal had been to bring about the epidemic of violence (the doubling of the murder rate, with corresponding increases in most categories of non-lethal violence) that followed the declaration of the "War on Drugs" in 1968, they could not have found a more effective method.

2 In Chapter 5, I described how effective higher education was in preventing further violence among prisoners in the Massachusetts prisons. But that was not the end of the story. Shortly after we had completed our original study, I reported the results in a public lecture at Harvard, and a copy of my lecture was given to the new Governor of Massachusetts, a former prosecutor who had been elected on the campaign promise to "reintroduce prisoners to the joys of busting rocks." Within days he stated in a press conference that we should abolish this program, otherwise people who could not afford to go to college would start committing crimes so they could go to prison and get a free college education! And he did succeed in effectively vitiating the program. Nor is this the behavior of one politician in one state: in 1997 the United States Congress repealed the Federal grant that provided the relatively

small funds for college textbooks and tuition for inmates in prisons throughout the country. So in the name of fighting crime and being tough on criminals we have systematically dismantled the single most effective program for enabling people to leave a life of crime and violence. The "War on Crime" is just as Orwellian a reversal of the plain meaning of the words of the English language as is the "War on Drugs."Indeed, all these slogans have their model in Orwell's 1984: "War is Peace," "Slavery is Freedom," etc.

3   It has been shown repeatedly that when the unemployment rate rises, the rates of homicide, suicide, imprisonment, mental hospitalization, and even deaths from natural causes all increase within a year or so; the causal mechanisms are not exactly mysterious. Yet for most of the past twenty years, whenever the unemployment rate decreased, the U.S. Federal Reserve Board would raise interest rates so as to increase the unemployment rate. This does not mean that they consciously intended to keep the rate of crime and violence as high as possible; but if that *had* been their intention, there is nothing they could have done that could have more surely increased the level of violence in the United States.

4   Repeated studies have found that when juveniles (children under the age of 18) are sent to adult prisons, they reoffend at higher rates than when they are sent to juvenile detention centers and are housed with other children. Yet the U.S. Congress and many state legislatures have passed laws mandating the transfer of juveniles to adult prisons. This is not to say that their purpose is to raise the recidivism rate to the highest possible level, but that is the effect of the laws they have been passing.

5   Repeated studies have found that the more severely children are punished, the more violent they become. Yet our courts and legislatures have continued to authorize the corporal punishment of children, the capital punishment of children, and so on.

6   Between 1984 and 1994, the rates of both committing homicide and being a victim of homicide tripled among 14–17-year-old American boys. This explosive increase in the murder rate was caused by one weapon only—the handgun. Yet the U.S. Congress and virtually every state

legislature refuses to outlaw the private possession and use of these weapons, and of the repeat-action assault rifles that are increasingly used in mass murders.

I think I have made my point: there is a complete and total disconnection between what most of our voters and government officials say they want to do (prevent violence) and what they actually do (stimulate violence). In order to make sense of this, I will mention another paradox, which I believe is related, namely, the fact that even though the wealth of the richest one per cent of Americans has skyrocketed since around 1968, while that of the middle class has stagnated, and for the poorest fractions of the population has actually declined, a majority of voters still vote for politicians who draw up tax and other laws that benefit the very wealthy and penalize everyone else. How are the wealthiest one per cent of the population able to persuade the other 99 per cent not merely to acquiesce in their own exploitation, but actually to support it through their votes? The United States is a democracy, most adults can vote, there is a free press—and yet people vote against their own plain rational self-interest!

There are undoubtedly several reasons for this, including the fact that the wealthiest one per cent own the mass media which tell people what to think, what to believe, who to vote for, and so on. (As someone said, the press is free—for anyone who owns one.) And the wealthiest individuals and corporations are the source of the campaign funds that are the prerequisite for running for political office in the United States, so that only a tiny minority of politicians can get elected without having to serve the interests of the very wealthy. But I would like to review evidence that it is not only that economic inequality stimulates violent crime; it is also true that increases in violent crime make it more politically feasible for the very wealthy to attain higher degrees of economic inequality (which is, of course, to their advantage by definition). For example, when I directed the Prison Mental Health Service, I noticed that in that microcosm of our society called the prison something similar was happening. The correction officers, who were vastly outnumbered by the inmates, realized that the inmates could together

easily overpower the officers and start a riot. How did the officers prevent that from happening? The simplest way for a minority to dominate a majority, and probably the most foolproof, is by the divide-and-
rule strategy. The officers let one group of inmates fight, dominate and
exploit another group—rape them, strong-arm them, steal from them,
and so on. The inmates were too busy fighting each other to unite
against the guards.

It is easy to see the similarity with the epidemic of violence in our
society. To illustrate what I mean, I will return to the comment made
by the former Governor of Massachusetts about free college education
for prison inmates. As long as higher education is not free, it is easy to
pit members of the lower middle class, who have to make painful sacrifices in order to go to college, against lower-class prison inmates for
whom that education is free. The fact that depriving prisoners of the
opportunity to acquire an education increases the rates of crime and
violence in our society, and that there is no reason a society as wealthy
as ours cannot afford to provide free higher education for everyone,
are points that tend to get lost in discussions of this issue.

But there are two even bigger points that also tend to get lost, so I
will emphasize them here. The first is that it is in the interests of the
extremely wealthy upper class for the government to pursue policies
whose effect is to raise the rates of crime and violence in our society. It
is in their economic interest to increase the gap between rich and the
poor to the highest level possible because they are the rich, and the
greater the gap, the more they get. But the larger that gap becomes, the
higher the rate of crime and violence. There is a clear conflict of interest between their economic interest in becoming wealthier, and the
public's interest in preventing violence.

There is also a political dimension: namely, how to persuade the
public to vote for politicians who will write the laws that keep diverting
more money into the hands of the upper class and out of the hands of
the middle and lower classes. A high rate of crime and violence pits
the middle class against the lower class. Most of the categories of violence that the laws define as criminal are committed by lower-class
people, and this makes the middle classes angry at the poor and afraid

of them. But it also divides the lower class against itself—most poor people do not commit violent crimes, but most of the victims of violent crime are poor. The higher the rates of crime and violence, then, the more the middle and lower classes are distracted from noticing that they are in most danger of being robbed by the very wealthy and their political agents. As the old saying goes, the poor man robs you with a gun, the rich man with a pen.

In this analysis, I am not assuming that there are many individual members of any class who are consciously aware of the role they are playing in this conflict. Some are, and of those, some work consciously to support this system, and some work consciously to oppose it. But the beauty of the system, from the standpoint of the rich, is that the vast majority of people whose lives are affected by it, whether for good or for ill, do not have to understand the system or consciously support it in order for it to work. The socio-economic and criminal justice systems do that job for them.

Representative strategists in both major American political parties are aware of these facts, and use them consciously in devising their political strategies. To take one example, Barry Goldwater's campaign manager in 1964 said that crime in America was a free multi-million dollar gift to the Republican Party. And as ex-President Bush's campaign strategist, Lee Atwater, put it, "Crime was a 'wedge issue'— to be driven into the Democratic Party in order to fragment it." (Sidney Blumenthal, "Crime Pays," *The New Yorker*, 9 May 1994.) "Representative Barney Frank, a liberal from Massachusetts and a member of the Judiciary Committee, says, 'There is an important political imperative: for the Republicans not to be able to accuse the Democrats of being soft on crime. Period. We have a dilemma— *division within the Party.*' (Ibid.)

Charles Schumer, then chairman of the House Subcommittee on Crime and Criminal Justice, referring to the Republican Party strategists, said, "They *want* a lot of criminals. The Republican Party only succeeds when the race issue is the divide. . . . When they try to win on non-race—abortion, gays—they lose. That's why they're going to crime. . . . That's when they win. They know it." (Ibid.)

Perceptive social scientists have long known this. As Christopher Jencks wrote in "Genes and Crime"(February 1987):

> Like rain on election day, crime is good for the Republicans. Whenever crime seems to be increasing, significant numbers of Americans tend to blame liberal permissiveness and turn to conservative political candidates, partly because they endorse a sterner approach to raising children, policing the streets, and punishing criminals, and partly because they oppose government "giveaways" to the poor, blacks, and other groups that commit a lot of crimes. While orthodox liberals answer that "getting tough" won't really help and that the way to reduce crime is to make society more just and opportunity more equal, this response to crime has seldom moved the electorate. When crime rates rise, liberals almost always find themselves on the defensive.

In "Solving Crime" (March 1986), Edgar Z. Friedenberg wrote that it is important to:

> demonstrate the ways in which crime *does* pay—not for criminals, but for certain elements in the community at large. . . . For dominant social groups it is an epiphenomenon that is costly mostly to lesser people whose lives are not so well-guarded, a side effect of the operation of the kinds of values that have made our capitalism effective. Eliminate violent crime? We couldn't leave home without it!

The political rhetoric of the ruling class claims to want to *decrease* the rate of violence. It advocates making the deadliest weapons, from handguns to assault rifles, freely available to as many people as possible; increasing the rate of capital punishment; imprisoning as many people as possible: and making the conditions in which they are incarcerated more and more brutalizing; depriving prison inmates of the opportunity to acquire education which could help them to renounce their criminal violence. All this is pursued in the name of being "tough on crime" and "tough on criminals"; but however "tough" these policies may be on criminals, they are, in fact, the most effective way to promote crime and violence. This deceptive rhetoric still fools millions of voters.

This brilliant strategy also labels those policies that *would* decrease the rates of crime and violence, as being "*soft* on crime." This is how "the Republicans have used the law-and-order issue for a generation to kneecap Democrats at will," as Sidney Blumenthal put it in "Crime Pays." "From the election of Richard Nixon through the election of George Bush, the Republicans held a strategic advantage on crime which was the domestic political equivalent of their advantage in foreign policy." The late President Lyndon Johnson understood how this system works. He described it as the "Bourbon strategy," referring to the white ruling class in the American South, the "Bourbons." He said that it was in their interest for racial prejudice to continue in the South. As long as the poor whites had even poorer blacks to look down on, they would not be as likely to resent the much greater wealth of the white upper class.

Human nature being what it is, people are more likely to pay attention to their own interest and to ignore the public interest. Nevertheless, many of the greatest leaders in the fight for both social and political democracy have been wealthy members of the ruling class who did not sacrifice the public interest to their class interests— Franklin Roosevelt, for example, was called a "traitor to his class" by many of his fellow plutocrats. And many rich individuals are generous with their wealth, establishing philanthropic foundations or donating to worthy causes. Of course, it is true that only the wealthy can afford to do this, and would not be rich in the first place if the collective wealth were more equitably shared. There would also then be no poor in need of their assistance. Help for the poor that depends on the arbitrary whims of the very rich, is shame-inducing for the poor, and too unreliable to guarantee their survival. But it is not useful to blame rich individuals for being rich, or for wanting to avoid the fate of the poor.

The social and economic structure of any given society can be seen as an ocean in which people are like so many fish who have to learn how to survive in that ocean or die. The ocean itself can be health-giving, fostering life for all the fish in it; or it can be a polluted ocean in which only the bigger and more powerful fish thrive, though there is always the risk that if it becomes too polluted even the big fish will perish. All social and economic systems in the world are somewhere on a continuum between those two extremes, though the current U.S. system, and the system in many developing and all undeveloping or regressing nations, approaches the most polluted extreme. In fact, the world system as a whole, with its division into a tiny minority of staggeringly wealthy nations and a great majority of increasingly poverty-stricken ones, can be considered extremely polluted. It is futile to blame individual big fish for surviving, or for wanting to survive.

So the point of this chapter is to emphasize that if we want to prevent violence, we will need to clean up this "ocean." We will need a system that as far as possible provides for an equal sharing of the collective wealth of the world among all individuals and all nations, while providing free education and healthcare for everyone. When the sharing comes close to being absolutely equal, as we have seen from examples at all stages of economic and cultural development, violence almost disappears. Conversely, the more unequal the social and economic environment, the more frequent and severe is the violence.

If we are to succeed, the political Orwellian Newspeak that surrounds us will have to be translated into plain English. Violence serves some very powerful interests. Those interests will continue to exist, and will continue to stimulate violence, until we eliminate the conflict of interest by eliminating the hierarchies and gender asymmetries.

One sign of a health-giving physical environment, one that is most supportive of individual life and survival, is the absence of physical pain. And one criterion by which to recognize an environment that is most conducive to the survival not only of individuals but also of groups, societies, and the whole species, is the absence of shame. The main precondition for preventing violence, then, is the establishment of the social and psychological conditions that minimize people's exposure to shame, and that maximize their access to non-violent means of undoing whatever shame they do experience, so that they can maintain their pride and self-esteem without doing so at the expense of the pride and self-esteem of others.

Select Bibliography and Sources

Adorno, T., E. Frenkel-Brunswik, D. J. Levinson and N. R. Sanford, *The Authoritarian Personality*, New York, 1950

Aghion, P., E. Caroli, and C. Gracia-Penalosa, "Inequality and Economic Growth," *Journal of Economic Literature*, 37 (4), 1999

Alexander, Franz, "Some Comments on the Relation between Guilt Feelings and Inferiority Feelings," *International Journal of Psychoanalysis*, vol. XX, 1938

Altemeyer, Bob, *The Authoritarian Specter*, Cambridge, Mass., 1996

American Friends Service Committee, *Inside the Walls: Control Units, Supermax Prisons, and Devices of Torture*, AFSC Briefing Paper, Philadelphia, Oct. 2000

Anderson, Elijah, *Code of the Street: Decency, Violence, and the Moral Life of the Inner City*, London and New York, 1999

Aviezer, O., M. H. Van Iizendoorn, A. Sagi, and C. Schuengel, "'Children of the Dream' Revisited: 70 Years of Collective Early Child Care in Israeli Kibbutzim," *Psychological Bulletin*, 116 (1), 1994

Benedict, Ruth, *Patterns of Culture* (1934), New York, 1958; London, 1961

—, *The Chrysanthemum and the Sword: Patterns of Japanese Culture*, New York, 1946; London, 1947

Berelson, Bernard and Gary A. Steiner, *Human Behavior*, New York, 1964

Bernstein, Jared and Ellen Houston, *Crime and Work*, Economic Policy Institute, Washington, D.C., July 2000

Bettelheim, Bruno, *The Children of the Dream*, London and New York, 1969

Black, Sir Douglas, J. N. Morris, Cyril Smith and Peter Townsend, *The Black Report*, published jointly with *The Health Divide*, P. Townsend, N. Davidson and M. Whitehead (eds), as *Inequalities in Health*, Harmondsworth, UK, 1992

Blumenthal, Sidney, "Crime Pays," *New Yorker*, 9 May, 1994

Boas, Franz, *General Anthropology*, Boston, Mass., 1938

Bok, Sissela, *Mayhem: Violence as Public Entertainment*, Reading, Mass., 1998

Braithwaite, John, *Inequality, Crime and Public Policy*, Boston, Mass., and London, 1979

Brenner, M. H., *Mental Illness and the Economy*, Cambridge, Mass., 1973

—, "Personal Stability and Economic Security," *Social Policy*, 8, 1977

Brown, Roger, *Social Psychology*, London and New York, 1965

Caulkins, Jonathan P., et al., *Mandatory Minimum Drug Sentences: Throwing Away the Key or the Taxpayers' Money?* Santa Monica, Calif., 1997

Centers for Disease Control, *Prevention of Youth Violence: A Framework for Community Action*, Atlanta, 1993

—, "Youth Violence Prevention," *American Journal of Preventive Medicine*, Supplement to vol. 12, No. 5, Sept./Oct. 1996

Chasin, Barbara, *Inequality and Violence in the United States*, Amherst, N.Y., 1998

Chiricos, Theodore, "Rates of Crime and Unemployment," *Social Problems*, 1987

Christie, Nils, *Crime Control as Industry: Towards GULAGS, Western Style?*, London and New York, 1993

Codere, Helen, *Fighting With Property*, New York, 1950

Currie, Elliott, *Confronting Crime: An American Challenge*, New York, 1985

Dar, Y., S. Kimhi, N. Stadler and A. D. Epstein, "The Imprint of the *Intifada*: Response of Kibbutz-Born Soldiers to Military Service in the West Bank and Gaza," *Armed Forces and Society*, 26 (2), Winter 2000

Dickinson, David, "Crime and Unemployment," University of Cambridge, Dept. of Applied Economics, 1993

Douglas, John, and Mark Olshaker, *The Anatomy of Motive: The FBI's Legendary Mindhunter Explores the Key to Understanding and Catching Violent Criminals*, New York, 1999

Downes, David, "Crime: Why Inequality Is Still a Factor," *Times Literary Supplement*, 1 Sept. 1995

Duke, Steven B., and Albert C. Gross, *America's Longest War: Rethinking Our Tragic Crusade Against Drugs*, New York, 1993

Eaton, Joseph W,. and Robert J. Weil, *Culture and Mental Disorders*, Glencoe, Ill., 1955

Engel, George L., "From biomedical to biopsychosocial: Being scientific in the human domain," *Psychosomatics* 1997 Nov.–Dec.; 38 (6)

Erikson, Erik H., *Childhood and Society,* (2nd edn) New York, 1963; (revised edn) Harmondsworth, U.K., 1965

Feshbach, S., "The Dynamics and Morality of Violence and Aggression," *American Psychologist,* 26, 1971

Fischer, Michael, and Brenda Geiger, *Reform Through Community: Resocializing Offenders in the Kibbutz,* London and New York, 1991

—, *Family, Justice, and Delinquency,* London and Westport, Conn., 1995

Frazier, Shervert H. (ed.), *Aggression* Association for Research in Nervous and Mental Disease, vol. 52, Baltimore, Md., 1974

Friedenburg, Edgar Z., "Solving Crime," *Journal of Reviews,* March 1986

Furby, Lita, "Satisfaction with Outcome Distributions: Studies from Two Small Communities," *Personality and Social Psychology,* 7 (2), 1981

Galbraith, James K., *Created Unequal: The Crisis in American Pay,* New York, 1998

Galtung, Johan, *Essays in Peace Research,* Copenhagen, 1975

Geen, R. G., "Effects of Frustration, Attack, and Prior Training in Aggressiveness upon Aggressive Behavior," *Journal of Personality and Social Psychology,* 9, 1968

Gibson, Thomas, "Raiding, trading, and tribal autonomy in insular Southeast Asia," in *The Anthropology of War,* J. Haas (ed.), Cambridge, U.K., 1990

Gilligan, James, *Violence: Our Deadly Epidemic and Its Causes,* New York, 1996; published in the U.K. as *Violence: Reflections on Our Deadliest Epidemic,* London, 2000

—, "Structural Violence," *Violence in America: An Encyclopedia,* (Ronald Gottesman Ed.-in-Chief) New York, 1999

—, "Punishment and Violence: Is the Criminal Law Based on One Huge Mistake?" *Social Research,* vol. 67, No. 3, Fall 2000

Glueck, Sheldon and Eleanor, *Unraveling Juvenile Delinquency,* New York, 1950

Glyn, Andrew and David Miliband (eds), *Paying for Inequality,* Concord, Mass., and London, 1994

Graubard, Stephen R. (ed.), *Health and Wealth,* Cambridge, Mass.: special issue of *Daedalus: Proceedings of the American Academy of Arts and Sciences,* vol. 123, Number 4, Fall 1994

Greenwood, Peter W., et al., *Diverting Children from a Life of Crime,* Santa Monica, Calif., 1996

Harris, Irving B., *Children in Jeopardy: Can We Break the Cycle of Poverty?,* New Haven, Conn., 1996

Hostetler, John A., *Hutterite Society,* Baltimore, Md., 1974; London, 1997

Hsieh, Ching-Chi and M.D. Pugh, "Poverty, Income Inequality, and Violent Crime," *Criminal Justice Review,* 18, 1993

James, Oliver, *Juvenile Violence in a Winner-Loser Culture,* London and New York, 1995

Jencks, Christopher, "Genes and Crime," *New York Review of Books,* 12 February 1987

Kaplan and Plaut, Thomas, *Personality in a Communal Society,* Lawrence, Kans., 1956

Keeley, Lawrence H., *War Before Civilization: The Myth of the Peaceful Savage,* New York, 1996

Kohn, Alfie, "Studies Find Reward Often No Motivator," *Boston Globe,* 19 Jan. 1987

Kohut, Heinz, *The Restoration of the Self,* New York, 1977

LeBlanc, Adrian Nicole, "The Outsiders: How the picked-on cope—or don't," *New York Times Magazine,* 22 August 1999

Levy, Jack, "Domestic Politics and War," in *The Origin and Prevention of Major Wars,* Robert I. Rotberg and Theodore K. Rabb (eds), New York, 1989

Luckenbill, David F., "Criminal Homicide as a Situated Transaction," *Social Problems,* 25 (2), 1977

Marans, Steven, et al., *The Police–Mental Health Partnership,* New Haven, Conn., 1995

Messner, Steven, "Income Inequality and Murder Rates: Some Cross-National Findings," *Comparative Social Research,* 1980

Miczek, Klaus A., et al., "Alcohol, Drugs of Abuse, Aggression, and Violence," in Reiss, Albert J. and Jeffrey A. Roth (eds), *Understanding and Preventing Violence,* vol. III, Washington, D.C., 1994

Mishel, Lawrence, Jared Bernstein and John Schmitt, *The State of Working America 2000–2001,* Economic Policy Institute Report, Ithaca, N.Y,, 2001

Myrdal, Gunnar, *Asian Drama: An Inquiry Into the Poverty of Nations*, Harmondsworth, UK, and New York, 1968

Newman, Katherine S., *No Shame in My Game: The Working Poor in the Inner City*, New York, 1999

Prothrow-Stith, Deborah, *Deadly Consequences: How Violence Is Destroying Our Teenage Population*, New York, 1993

Reiss, Albert J. and Jeffrey A. Roth (eds), *Understanding and Preventing Violence*, vol. 1, Washington, D.C., 1993

Richardson, L. F., *Statistics of Deadly Quarrels*, London and Pittsburgh, Pa., 1960

Ryan, William, *Equality*, New York, 1981

Rochlin, Gregory, *Man's Aggression: The Defense of the Self*, Boston, Mass., and London 1973

Russell, Bertrand, *Roads to Freedom*, London, 1918

Sabini, John, "Aggression in the Laboratory," in Kutash, I. L., S. B. Kutash and L. B. Schlesinger (eds), *Violence*, San Francisco, 1978

Scheff, Thomas and Suzanne Retzinger, *Emotions and Violence: Shame and Rage in Destructive Conficts*, Lexington, Mass., 1991

Schmitt, John, "Why Should Europe Follow Our Lead?" *New York Times*, 25 Aug. 1999

Sears, R. R., J. W. M. Whiting, V. Nowlis and P. S. Sears, "Some Child-Rearing Antecedents of Aggression and Dependency in Young Children," *Genetic Psychology Monographs* 47, 1953

Sears, R. R., E. E. Maccoby and H. Levin, *Patterns of Child Rearing*, Evanston, Ill., 1957

Sedlock, A. J. and D. D. Broadhurst, *Executive Summary of the Third National Incidence Study of Child Abuse and Neglect* (NIS-3), Washington, D.C., 1996

Sen, Amartya, *Development as Freedom*, New York, 1999

Sherman, Lawrence W., et al. (eds), *Preventing Crime: What Works, What Doesn't, What's Promising: A Report to the United States Congress Prepared for the National Institute of Justice*, Washington, D.C., February 1997

Short, James F. Jr., *Poverty, Ethnicity, and Violent Crime*, Boulder, Conn., and Oxford, 1997

Silberman, Charles E., *Criminal Violence, Criminal Justice*, New York, 1978

Smeeding, Timothy M., "Financial Poverty in Developed Countries: The Evidence From the Luxembourg Income Study," in *Human Development Papers 1997: Poverty and Human Development*, New York: UN Development Programme, 1997

Smith, Dan, *War, Peace and Third World Development*, New York: UN Development Programme, 1994

Smith, M. Dwayne, and Margaret A. Zahn (eds), *Studying and Preventing Homicide: Issues and Challenges*. Thousand Oaks, Calif., 1999—*see especially* Gary LaFree, "Homicide: Cross-National Perspectives."

—, *Homicide: A Sourcebook of Social Research*, Thousand Oaks, Calif., 1999

Spiegel, Dina, and Judith L. Alpert, "The relationship between shame and rage: Conceptualizing the violence at Columbine High School," *Journal for the Psychoanalysis of Culture & Society*, vol 5 (2), 2000

Spiro, Melford, *Kibbutz: Venture in Utopia* (augmented edn), Cambridge, Mass., 1975

Straus, Murray A., and Richard J. Gelles, "Societal Change and Change in Family Violence from 1975 to 1985," *Journal of Marriage and the Family*, 48, 1986

Textor, Robert, *A Cross-Cultural Summary*, New Haven: Human Relations Area Files, 1967

Thomas, Herbert E., "Experiencing a Shame Response as a Precursor to Violence," *Bulletin American Academy of Psychiatry and Law*, 23 (4)

Tolan, Patrick and Nancy Guerra, *What Works in Reducing Adolescent Violence*, Boulder, Conn., Institute of Behavioral Science, 1998

Tonry, Michael H. and David P. Farrington (eds), *Building a Safer Society: Strategic Approaches to Crime Prevention* (Crime and Justice, vol. 19), Chicago, Ill., 1995

UN Development Programme, *United Nations Human Development Report 1998*, New York, 1998

Weart, Spencer R., *Never at War: Why Democracies Will Not Fight One Another*, London and New Haven, Conn., 1998

Wilkinson, Richard G., *Unhealthy Societies: The Afflictions of Inequality*, London and New York, 1996

Wolff, Edward N., in *Top Heavy: The Increasing Inequality of Wealth in America and What Can Be Done about It*, New York, 1996

Wolfgang, Marvin E., *Patterns in Criminal Homicide* (1958), New York, 1966

INDEX

African-Americans: criminal violence and
88–9; in the U.S. caste system 46–7
age discrimination 47–9
alcohol, violence and 112
Alexander, Franz 30
Alger, Horatio 44–5
American Friends Service Committee, *Inside
the Walls* (report) 123
American high school massacres 68–75
Amish, The 86
amnesty policies 8
Anabaptist communities 86–7
Anderson, Elijah, Philadelphia fieldwork 34–5
Aquinas, Thomas 31
Aristotle 31, 33, 103
Asia: revolutionary violence 44; violence
towards women 60–1
authoritarianism: individuals 35, 55; lack of in
kibbutzim 87; political structures 54–5

Benedict, Ruth 50–1, 55
Bettelheim, Bruno 88
Black Report, The 21
Boas, Frank 51
Brandeis, Louis (Justice) 93

Cain and Abel 30–1
California, studies of murder in (1963–72) 34
caste *see* social class
censorship, of media violence 95–6
child abuse 49, 61, 64; a cause of future
violence 36, 64, 110–11; sexual 130;
in single-parent families 77–8
children: corporal punishment 48, 87, 132;
drugs and 111–12; violence towards 94, 132
circumcision, female and male 62
classless societies 86–8, 89–91
Cohen, Donald 109
Columbine High School massacre (Colorado)
71–5
communities, violence prevention 9–11
community policing 110
community service 129
confession of sins 51–2
conscience 51
criminal courts 22, 23; alternative sentencing
models 129–30, *see also* justice
criminal law, basis of questioned 12–18

democracy: social and political 83–6, 91, 108;
and war 54–5

Democratic Party (U.S.A.) 135, 137
Douglas, John, F.B.I. "profiler" 35
drugs: drug courts 129; violence and 111–13,
131, *see also* substance abuse

economic interests 24
education: and media violence 95, 96; in
prisons 98–9, 119, 127, 131–2, 134; and self-
esteem 98–9
educational programs 109, 119, 127
Eisenhower, Dwight D. 84
employment *see* unemployment; work
ethnic cleansing 8
evil, concept of 14; in shame cultures 52

families: domestic violence 55, 109, 111;
single-parent 77–9, 108
firearms *see* guns
Freud, Sigmund 65, 87
frustration, aggressive behavior and 32–3

Galbraith, James K., 40–2, 43
gender roles 58–62, 63, 65; homophobia and
92–3; violence and 38–9, 56–65
genocide 8, 27, 28
ghettos, inner-city 34–5, 73
Goldwater, Barry 135
guilt cultures 49–50, 51–54
gun control 96–8, 132–3
guns, possession of 46, 97, 132–3, 136

Harris, Eric 71–3
Hegel, Georg Wilhelm Friedrich 31
Hennessey, Michael, San Francisco Sheriff
126
Hitler, Adolf 53, 85
homicide rates: gun possession and 97, 98,
132–3; unemployment and 92, 132; world
comparisons 39, 83–6
homophobia 62–5, 68; gender roles and
92–3; harassment 70, 71
"homosexual panic" 64
house arrest 129
Human Relations Area Files 53–4
hunter-gatherer communities 89–91
Hutterites 54, 86–7

immigrants, criminal violence and 88–9
incest 61
infidelity, in marriage 61
injustice, feeling a victim to 33, 101

insult, cause of aggression 31–4, 57–8
International Criminal Tribunal (The Hague) 8

Japan: inequities of wealth and income 39, 78; single-parent families 78
Jefferson, Thomas 104
Johnson, Lyndon B. 137
justice 7; alternative sentencing models 129–30; restorative 8, 126, 129; retributive 8, 129, see also criminal courts

Keynes, John Maynard 85
kibbutzim 87–8
Klebold, Dylan 71–2, 73
Kwakiutl Indians 50–1

leisure, and work 103
Littleton (Colorado), high school massacre 69, 71–5
Luckenbill, David 34

machismo 63, 65
Major, John 101
Malcolm X 75
Marans, Steven 109
Marcum, Michael, San Francisco Assistant Sheriff 126
martyrdom 50, 52
Marx, Karl 31–2, 33, 100
masculinity: prison discussions program 126–7; shame and 57–8, 67–8; violence and 38–9, 56–65, 66–8, see also men
masochism 50
mass murders 68–75
media violence, restriction of 84–6
men: as "violence objects" 59, 60, 62, see also masculinity
Mennonites 86
mental health clinics, in prisons 16–17
mental illness, violence and 15–17, 42
Myrdal, Gunnar 44

"neo-Nazis" 55

pacifist societies 86, 89–91
paedophilia and paedophiles 61, 130
paranoia, and homophobia 64–5
Paterson, Sir Alexander 125
patriarchal societies 56, 59, 60, 61, 65, 68
penance 53
Philadelphia, ghetto fieldwork 34–5
Plato 103
Police–Mental Health Partnership (1995) 109–10

political interests, and violence 24, 26–7, 133, 134–8
poverty, relative: correlation with violent crime 39–46, 66–7; elimination of 101–2; single-parent families and 78
prevention of violence: community initiatives 9–11; moral and legal approach 7, 12, 17–18; in prisons 16–17, 22, 23, 117–28; public health and preventive medicine approach 14, 16–17, 18–25; punishment and 22; secondary programs (interventions) 21–2, 107–13; societal change and 81–106; tertiary (therapeutic) prevention 8, 22–4, 99, 114–30, see also violence
pride: violence and 29–37; without violence 138
prisons: anti-prisons 117–19, 129; conjugal visits and furloughs 128–9; education programs 98–9, 119, 127, 131–2; ineffectuality of 117; prevention of violence 16–17, 22, 23, 117–28; "supermax" 122–3; violence in 13–17, 61–2, 63–5, 117, 127
productivity, wealth and income equalization and 106
punishment 7, 14, 17–18, 23, 87; capital punishment 94, 132, 136; corporal punishment 48, 87, 132; guilt cultures and 52–3; prevention of violence and 22, 115–17

racial discrimination 8
RAND Corporation: drugs and crime report 113; prevention of violence program 107–8
rape 61, 63; male rape 61–2, 64
recidivism 99
recognition, desire for 31
rejection 32, 69, 71–2
Republican Party (U.S.A.), and the crime issue 135–7
respect: for prisoners 120–2, 123; and shame 53, 72–5, 80–1; violence and 29, 31, 34, 35–6, 70–7
restraint, of violent persons 116, 123–6
Roosevelt, Franklin D. 92, 137
Russell, Bertrand 19, 104

San Francisco, violence prevention program 126–8
Schwartz, Sunny 126
self-esteem see pride
Sen, Amartya 100
sentencing practices, alternative 129–30
sex, extra or premarital 61
sexual adequacy/inadequacy, masculinity and 67–8, 76

sexual promiscuity: in men 63; in women 58

Shakespeare, William 53, 95, 100

shame: inequity and 99–100, 137; masculinity and 57–8; single-parent families and 79; unemployment and 75–7; violence and 29–37, 38, 43–4, 46, 47, 48, 52–4, 66–8, 69, 72–5, 138

shame cultures 49–54

Shaw, George Bernard 59

Silberman, Charles E. 88

sin 51–2, 87

Sinclair, Hamish 126

single-parent families 77–9, 108

slave labor 103–4

slavery 54

Smith, Adam 100

social class 38, 43–4, 54, 104; in America 45, 46–7; among Hutterites 86; correlation with violence 66–7, 69, 73–5, 134–5; in kibbutzim 87–8; societal change and 81–3

social democracy 83–6, 108

social mobility, in the U.S. and Europe 45

societal change, and prevention of violence 81–106

Straus, Murray A. 55

street culture 34–5

substance abuse 23, 129, see also drugs

suicide 50, 52, 72–3, 84, 87, 92

survival, of human societies 26–7

Sweden: inequities of wealth and income 39, 78; single-parent families 78–9

taxation: voter self-interest and 133; wealth taxes 102–3

Third World countries 106; homicide rates 39

"three-strikes" law 108

tobacco 112

Tolstoy, Count Leo 104

"Trenchcoat Mafia" 71

"truth and reconciliation commissions" 8

unemployment: shame and 75–7; violent crime and 39–46, 91–2, 132

United Kingdom, inequities and homicide rates 39, 40, 41

United Nations 8; Human Development Report 1998 82

United Nations Committee Against Torture 14, 123

United States: criminal justice system 14–15, 18, 22–4, 114–16, 135; Federal Reserve Board 92, 132; health care 23; inequities and violent crime 39, 40–3, 45, 78–9, 132–3; single-parent families 108; social democracy and 83–4; unemployment and violence 42–3, 132

United States Constitution, Second Amendment 97, 98

University of Colorado (Boulder), Center for the Study and Prevention of Violence 9

Versailles, Treaty of (1919) 53, 85

victims of violence: concern for 24; confrontation meetings 127

violence: causes of 12, 14, 20; cultural differences 49–54; as a disease 19–20; domestic 55, 109, 111; eliminating structural violence 101–2; masculinity and 38–9, 56–65, 66–8; psychological causes of 29–37, 66–7; risk factors 66–7, 68; social causes of 38–55, 66–7, see also prevention of violence

violent behavior, at risk groups 21–2, 66–7, 68

virginity, gender and 60

war 27, 48–9, 54–5, 56, 58, 59, 83, 84–6, 89

war crimes 8, 18

Washington, George 104

wealth: and greed 134; redistribution of 24, 82, 102–3, 105–6, 137

welfare dependency 79

welfare state see social democracy

Winnicott, D. W. 126

women: honor and 56, 57–62; as "sex-objects" 59, 60, 61; violence and 58–9

Woolf, Virginia 57, 58

work, and leisure 103–5

World War I 83; peace settlement 85

World War II 83; peace settlement 85–6

Yale University, Child Study Center 109

youth: criminal behavior 109; violence and 48–9, 66–7